Are you financially Asleep or Awake?

With Bonus Chapters

Friday M. Simfukwe

ARE YOU FINANCIALLY ASLEEP OR AWAKE
A book about how money drives your purpose in life
Copyright © 2010 by Friday M. Simfukwe
www.walola.com

Published by CreateSpace
100 Enterprise Way
Suite A200
Scotts Valley, CA 95066

ISBN 1453757279
EAN-13 9791453757277

Book cover design by Cyanide Design
All illustrations done by Paulus Farrell
All scripture quotations, unless otherwise stated, are taken from the
Holy Bible, King James Version

Printed in the USA
First Published October 2010

Contents

Contents

Contents

Acknowledgments

I would like to thank my Lord Jesus Christ who has given me inspiration and insight on the subject of money and how it relates to a man's purpose and future on this earth. There is no one on this planet who can boast that what they have was entirely a result of their sweat; everything we are and everything we own is all but a gift from above for which personally I am eternally grateful.

To my dear wife Tricia, this book wouldn't have made it without your unfailing support and the faith you have in me – you will be greatly rewarded.
I would also like to thank my children Billy and Salifya for their patience and support during the time I was scribbling these thoughts in my diaries; I love you guys dearly.

My bishop and father, Bishop George Mbulo – Senior Pastor Capital Christian Worship Center and mom Rev. B, you have been a great inspiration not only to me as an individual, but to my family as a whole – am forever indebted to you.

Finally to my readers and all those who have generously contributed to the publication of this book unknowingly, I say thank you and may this book indeed be a blessing to you.

Foreword

Are you financially Asleep or Awake is a treatise that compels you to take stock of the state of your mind with its consequent outcomes that engulf your life on earth. The author deals with a subject matter that is not for the fainthearted, for they will swiftly eschew it; but the daring and valorous will unequivocally embrace it as they gallantly pursue what God intended for them to be in our world.

As you pick up this book to read, you will be challenged to consider the unavoidable question of your thought pattern or mind-set. You will discover that your mind is the most critical and pivotal area of a *make or break* confrontation to your life's purpose. It's an inescapable fact that money occupies a cardinal part of our earthly and human enterprise; but money, and the power of money, as the author clearly demonstrates, if not perceived correctly, can enslave one's life. It's the mastery of money that we should strive for, as this will put us at the top where God intended for us to be. The author shows you how you can become master and not a slave to money.

When a human mind is incarcerated in the maze of social or cultural complexes that impose limitations on the God-given premonition and drive to be at the top or become successful in life, such as racism, utilitarian exploitation, etc., a person settles for the bare minimum and capitulates to the *survival of the fittest* mentality. This inevitably births a dichotomy of apprehension of the mind on one hand, as it struggles to accept the status quo of a diminished capacity which is foreign to it, and on the other hand the reality of living in this world which requires one to have capacity to successfully meet life's needs.

You are either financially Awake or you may be someone that is financially Asleep, depending on how you've dealt with your mind-set. The battle for your mind is what the author endeavors to sensitize you to, and he implores you to consequently seek for a triumphal ascendancy of your mind. You are being challenged to avoid a cursory look at the matter of wealth verses poverty. The subject of wealth acquisition demands critical and serious consideration of the driving force, which is your mind. You will either rise or fall depending on the state of your mind towards what God has purposed you to be. The correct realigning of your thought patterns, that is your mind, with what God has endowed upon you individually and uniquely, will spur you into your full potential to live a fulfilled and successful life.

Go on and dare to read this material you have in your hands right now. Approaching it with an open, and truly searching, mind that will not settle for the normal, but will reach for the unusual, which is the domain of the great achievers of our world. The author has forewarned you that he makes reference to biblical principles, but this is not intended to be a religious treatise. Therefore, hold your horses on unfairly juxtaposing this book with some commonly espoused religious concepts. The principles the author has so ably outlined in this book will help your cause to becoming what God intended for you to be in this life.
You were meant to be financially Awake!

Bishop George Mbulo

A tribute to my mother - *May her soul rest in peace*

Deep in the woods of a small township called Butondo, in Mufulira, Zambia, a thirty eight year old woman lay on her death-bed with an asthma attack that had characterized her life for over fifteen years.

"*Monje!! Monje!!*" my father called out to mom as he helplessly watched her gasp for breath in pain. She tried to open her eyes and utter something to her husband, but she was too weak to even open her eyes. Air seemed to have run out on her. Suddenly, she felt herself slip into unconsciousness as she silently committed her spirit in the hands of her maker.

The Ronald Ross hospital ambulance was just about late to pick up my mother from her home at house No. A90 Butondo township. Medical personnel hurriedly put the body of my mother on a stretcher not wanting to make it a police case should they certify her dead on arrival. They fired off the ambulance siren and sped off to the hospital.

For some God-ordained reasons, nurses and other medical attendants were more compassionate those days; the ambulance was full of them and they worked over-time, trying to resuscitate the life of my mother, as the ambulance "*sirened away*".

This was two years before I was born; my mom narrated to me that during this gruesome experience, she however, was completely awake in another world where she saw a man standing before her with a jar of water in his hands. "*take it and drink*" the man said to her. When she took the drink, the man then said "*your life is not over yet*".

The medical doctors could not believe it when suddenly, they heard mom, in her hospital bed, cough as she opened her eyes before them. They had almost given up and were ready to prepare the death certificate. She felt no pain any more and her breathing was normal again. Her doctor wanted to keep her a few days in hospital for observation, but she insisted that she was ready to go home.

My parents were advised at this point, to not have another child again for the safety and life of my mother. My immediate elder sister, Maureen, was to be their last born child in a family of seven children. *Ventolin* became my mother's daily medicine and she was not to move without an inhaler.

"Accidentally" as my ninth grade English teacher would say, my mother conceived again; and in fear, she vowed never to do this ever again; only if the gracious would grant her successful delivery as well as spare her life just this once.

Well, little did she know that her last born baby boy was really not an accident at all, but a re-organization of the universe to make sure that my birth was necessitated through her so that you could today, read this book which I believe will help you to see things from a perception of purpose - and not of fate or of accidents.

My mother went on to live for another twenty two years after my birth and then she passed on.

I dedicate this book to the memory of the woman that was used to bring me into this earth *Edina Namonje Simfukwe.*

Are you financially Asleep or Awake?

Introduction

This book is not entirely just all about money as the title may suggest; our modern day society is a fast track society where everyone is racing towards financial freedom but yet neglects and ignores the real reasons for attaining such financial freedom. Why do you want to be financially free? Why do you need all that money? Why is the whole world in a hurry to acquire wealth? Hundreds of sermons in church today are about money and prosperity; many books have been written about financial success and how to acquire great wealth, yet not everyone who reads these books attains the promises that these books give.

This book is a treasure repository of nuggets of truth that can completely transform your destiny. It's about living a life completely driven by purpose. It's a road map to greatness. It will show you how you can become master over money and not let it master you. It will open your understanding of how money affects your future and destiny and will clearly light this path for your own life.

Some may find this book quite controversial on certain issues; I must straight away, inform you that although this book takes a biblical point of view on the subject of money, it is not a *religious* book and may therefore upset and challenge some of your religious beliefs and paradigms.

If you are not ready to stand out in this world, if you are not ready to be unique and influential, if you are not ready to be original, if you are not ready to be yourself and make history, then don't read this book, because it might leave you with a feeling of guilt for not making choices in your life that are crucial for the benefit of this world and indeed for your own.

You were not meant to live life as a nonentity and pass on insignificantly – there is a greatness trapped inside you that can only be shown to the world when you make the right choices in your life.

You are so unique that you were not meant to fit in or blend into society to only be counted among the crowd; your future will not come to you, you need to go there. It has been said that your life today is a sum total of all your past choices up to this point.

So many people live in a cycle of life and do not realize that their lives are a continuous repetition of boring activities that do not lead them to their future.

Albert Einstein said: *"Doing the same things over and over and expecting different results, is the definition of insanity."*

No! You were meant to stand out and not blend in, you were meant to be above average not to be "normal" you were meant to be a master and not a slave – but you cannot be master by default; you need to make certain choices and execute certain decisions to make it as a master; however, you cannot make these choices and execute these decisions unless you think in a certain way, not like *"normal"* people think; because the value of your life, lies within your thoughts.

The decision you made to get your hands on this piece of literature may become one of the greatest investments of your time ever made regarding the shaping of your purpose driven life.

Average people are people who are content with living from

paycheck to paycheck, from one debt to another debt, and religiously wait for that pension and retirement benefit when their days are finally over.

Average people are people who do not give a thought about how their influence can penetrate the world but rather live under someone else's influence.

Average people are people who care less about making a difference, but rather adapt to the environments in which they live.

Average people are people who always have someone else to blame for their misfortunes, but they themselves do nothing in training of their minds to shape their destinies.

If this is how you see your life and you do not perceive much beyond these boundaries, but would like a more exciting and influential life, then read on.

I have not put down ink on the pages of this book simply to excite your emotions and make some additions to your knowledge base, I'm appealing to your *genius* trapped inside you; yes you heard me right; there is a genius trapped inside you who needs a little stirring to bring out your greatness. I'm here to inform you that you were not meant to die a follower, but a world class leader; however, this is entirely dependent on the choices you make.

This entire world is only controlled by two great masters and it's not God and the Devil.

Jesus Christ once said: "*No man can serve two masters: for either he will hate the one, and love the other; or else he will hold to the one, and despise the other. Ye cannot serve God and mammon.*" Mat 6:24.

The word '*mammon*' is also translated '*money*' or '*wealth*'. At this instance, Jesus was communicating that the only true opponent to God was money and not the devil.

The bible also says: *"For the love of money is the root of all evil which while some coveted after, they have erred from the faith, and pierced themselves through with many sorrows. "*1 Tim 6:10.

People have been made to believe that the devil is the root or the source of all evil and so all evil activities are blamed on the devil; however, the bible which they 'quote' says another thing all together; the love of money is the source, the beginning or the foundation of all evil. Money itself is not evil; it's the love for it that is evil because it shifts you away from your true purpose in life.

Anybody can preach against the love of money; but what is the love of money? How can you tell if you have the love for money or not?
Everyone wakes up early in the morning to go and work in order to earn money; everything you do is somehow somewhere connected to money, so how can you distinguish between genuine commitment to life and the love of money?

Having the love for money does not mean being emotionally attached to those pieces of paper imprinted with dead men's faces; it does not mean loving the way the pieces of paper have been decorated and adoring their scent. Money is simply a representation of the value of a thing. Therefore, to love money is to love the worldly things it can acquire. When the bible talks about the love of money, it is referring to a character that covets worldly acquisitions. It is this character that causes you to steal from your brother because of the lust of your eyes and the pride of life that money can supposedly buy for you. Man has not realized the power behind money and has therefore been literally enslaved by it without knowing. The result of this worldwide ignorance about money has caused the whole world to faithfully and religiously work for money all their lives. Instead of being master, the world has let money be master and has allowed it to rule their lives.

Being financially awake is being placed on the level of master of money, so you can have the time to fulfil your God-given dreams in your life time.
You only have one life on this earth, and you can't afford to spend it all working to earn a living; working for money year after year.
Most people's dream is to become wealthy so that they can be called *rich;* however, this passion is due to lack of understanding of purpose. Even though wealth is a necessity in life, it should not be your goal. Having such a goal will enslave you and make you a perpetual subject to money.

Open your mind as you go through the pages of this book. Don't chain yourself to doctrines and teachings that will kill your genius rather than give it life, release your spirit and allow it to soar like the eagle that it is!!

Chapter 1

Knowledge is more powerful than color

Destroying the myth behind 'cultural' poverty

*T*he ugly birth of racism among different races has brought about a destiny killing complex that unfortunately still lives deep in the minds of many people to this day. No matter how much we try to either pretend or ignore its existence, the spirit of racism is very much alive among our societies and cultures.

Perpetrated, unfortunately, by an institution that should have been fighting against it, racism has been the biggest blow to a man's confidence and identity.

Traces of this vice can be found among people of different ethnic cultures (the blacks against the whites, the Arabs against the Jews, Asians against those among their own with different shades of skin color, the poor against the rich and so on...) but the biggest has been between white people and black people or should we say the lighter skinned races against the darker skinned races.

For centuries, white people had been taught and trained that they are a superior race to the blacks, and black people, through the slave trade that resulted from this teaching, have also been taught and trained that they are inferior to the white race. This brain-washing has been so deep seated that to progress beyond this point; we will need a re-brain-washing in the right way, literally a retraining of our minds.

It's not an easy job to simply tell someone, who has gone through this brain washing and thinks that anything black is bad while everything white is good, to tell them that there is nothing wrong with black, would almost take a rebirth of their mind to accept. Some people actually attribute the underdevelopment of Africa to the color of the skin of the African man.

Is the poverty in Africa inherent in the black man's skin? Is the black man under a curse to live in perpetual poverty?

From my childhood, whenever I saw the picture of the devil, he was painted black, and Jesus was always painted white skinned. All the angels in my junior bible stories book were white, while their counterparts, the demons, were all black. The English language even has terminologies such as: "*black sheep*", meaning "a member of a family or group who is considered undesirable or disreputable – really a disgrace".

Some of the meanings of phrases used with the word "*black*" as quoted from the American Heritage Dictionary of the English Language are as follows and I quote:

"*Black deeds*" means: evil and wicked deeds.
"*Black thoughts*" means: cheerless and depressingly gloomy thoughts.
"*He gave me a black look*" means: his look was marked by anger and sullenness.
"*A black day*" means: a day full of disaster and calamity.

Other phrases used with the word "*white*" are as follows and I quote:

"*That's very white of you.*" Means you are decent, honorable and dependable.
"*White magic*" is magic that is without malice and harmless.
"*White*" also means auspicious and fortunate, morally pure and innocent.
To "*black out*" means to lose consciousness while to "*white out*" means to correct errors. The list goes on and on.

With this background from infancy, reprogramming your mind to think differently is not an easy bit.
Our society has been staged to uplift the white race and down tread the black race. This is why slave trade was considered "*normal*", the black man was not regarded as a complete human, and this was even preached in church. The church which was supposed to fight the scourge was actually in the forefront promoting this evil act in the name of the Lord.

To this day, when an indigenous black man sees a white man, he feels like he has met an object worth of respect because he's been trained to think that way; that the white man is above him; and likewise, the white man feels superior when in the presence of a black man. Many white men were taught and trained that the black man is supposed to work for them and not the other way round.

When I was growing up, whenever I did something that my mom liked, she showered me with praises, and this is how she'd go:
"*Oh what a brilliant boy you are, you are a child of a white man ("uli mwana wamusungu!!*" In my own indigenous tongue), you are a

white man, and your skin deceives us all!!" …and she'd go on and on bragging about how "white" I was and I'd feel really great and proud.

On the other hand, when I messed up, black was all over me; *"you black African boy, what's wrong with you??"* she'd scream; this was the time you hated to be black. I wasn't the only one, who had this experience in my childhood, but this upbringing unconsciously trains you that to be black is an unfortunate consequence; you should have been born white. Apart from the slave trading of black people of Africa, those that escaped and remained in their countries were subjected to the tragic effects of colonialism. The segregation, the mistreatment and torture from this *epidemic* further cemented the inferior complexes in the minds of the black people.

Their lives became wholly dependent on the colonial masters that ruled them for years.

And when they could no longer manage themselves without the help of their masters, they were finally given the so called *independence.*

You cannot be truly independent until your thinking is independent. The black people of Africa were colonized to think like their masters wanted, to speak the language of their masters, to think that they were not able to rule themselves, they were colonized to think that their masters were smarter than them. They were trained to depend on their masters, and when this was eventually enshrined in their black minds, they got their *independence.*

In essence, the black man in Africa got his independence when he could no longer rule himself effectively. To this day, Africa is still struggling with issues of governance and poverty, not because Africa has no resources, but primarily because it does not have a mind of its own. Africa still economically depends on its colonial masters to a very large extent; the amount of international debt accumulated in many African countries is a direct indication of this dependence and inability for Africa to rule herself effectively. Africa still has its master in the white man; and Africa lives by the economic policies propagated by its master.

However, in spite of all this, you cannot continue to blame the past for your present and your future *misdemeanor*.
As a people, we need to squarely deal with this before we can make significant progress towards our own emancipation.
Black people need to know that having an inferior perception of oneself will always cause your mind to function at below average. White people do not have a problem here, it's the black man that has been looked down upon as having a below average brain, inferior to the white man's brain. An inferior self image will always result into an inferior lifestyle.

However, this does not exclude the fact that even a white man can have an inferior complex resulting from the effects of his background or the environment he finds himself in.

To a person with this mind-set, it would take a total transformation of their mind to understand that there is no difference between a black man and a white man except the color of their skin.

Unfortunately, your subconscious mind will always resist change from its prior training and customs; this is a protection mechanism working in your system. Every person is either brain washed by them selves or by the environment in which they live to believe and think in a certain way.

Brain washing can either be positive or negative. There are numerous positive confession materials around to help change the belief system and mind-set of an individual; however, this alone would not completely help to uninstall an inferior mind-set that's been established in a life for a long time.

The mind naturally rejects any statement it receives that otherwise violates its prior training or belief system. For instance, think about your mother for a while; how tender and kind she has been to you in bringing you up to where you are, caring for you in all your intolerable behaviors. Now imagine that if for some reason, you have just been told that the woman you have always called and known to be your mother since your childhood is actually not your mother.....

Already, your mind cannot wrap itself around this because it cannot find any immediate replacement and it therefore creates a conflict to this statement

Apart from the trauma that this might cause, which of course is due to the conflict that the mind initiates, getting to a stage where you actually accept and believe that the woman is not your mother, will require a great deal of retraining your mind, unless of course she was a bad mother, but even then, you'll have a lot of *hail* to accept the change.

It is however, interesting to note that the mind does not create a conflict when approached with a question. It immediately begins a process of searching for an appropriate answer. Whether it arrives at a solution or not, is not the point, but the mechanisms to smoothly reach a conclusion are set in motion without a conflict.

Let's imagine, using the scenario we had about our mother, that you ask yourself this question: *"is this woman my mother?"* What you have done is: you have not given your mind any contradicting statements about what you believe but rather confronted it with an objective question about what you believe. You have not given it a final conclusive statement, but asked it to question its prior training. What the mind will do in this case is begin a process to prove that what it believes is in fact true.

It's during this process, that you need to feed your mind with facts that will lead it to a true conclusion.

This is the quickest way to retrain your mind to think differently. The less you know, the more vulnerable you'll become.

Please don't ask your mother whether she's your mother, because she is.

In this information era that we have found our selves in, information is what separates between the 'well to do' and the "can't make ends meet" between the rich and the poor; not the color of your skin.

The internet has become the greatest equalizer of all time, information that was once not available to you, is now available to all; strive to get knowledge.

'Therefore, my people are gone into captivity, because they have no knowledge and their honorable men are famished and their multitude dried up with thirst." Isaiah 5:13

The greatest enemy to your success; to your business, to your academics and any other sector of your life is not the color of your skin but "ignorance".

Ignorance of what works and when it works; ignorance of the correct policies to adopt in a nation or in your life; ignorance of who you are!! Yearn for knowledge.

The text from Isaiah 5:13 above, implies that the main reason you are hungry and in bondage is that you have no knowledge.

Most of Africa fits this description perfectly; *into captivity and famished.*

Because Africa, in general, does not have a culture of reading, this prevents the creation of a pool of knowledge within the continent. When slaves were taken from Africa, they were forbidden from learning to read and write, lest they discovered themselves and knew what their masters knew. Have you ever heard of the phrase…

If you want to hide anything from a black man, put it in a book…??

Knowledge will give you power to face your future with confidence.

Knowledge will break down those chains of inferior complexes resulting from racism and segregation.

Knowledge will set you apart and create you a throne.

Knowledge will give you wings to fly above your circumstances.

Knowledge will illuminate your mind and cause you to have something to smile about.

Knowledge is the key to your greatness

Knowledge is more powerful than color!!

But what is knowledge?

True knowledge is one that starts from knowing yourself first. Even a prince, if he does not know that he is a prince, he will live like a slave. Knowing yourself will direct the course of your life and will determine what you touch, what you study and eventually what you achieve. However, you can never truly know yourself without first knowing your source. If you do not know where you are coming from, you will not know where you are going – and this is truly tragic.

What would be the point of you spending five years in the school of engineering studying *Mechanical Engineering* when you know for sure that your passion is law and nothing will make you happier than you becoming a lawyer? It is not about what your father or uncle wants you to be, it's what makes you who you are.

Unfortunately, there is no college nor university in the world that offers a course about you and who you are; the greatest university that offers that course is inside you; attend that course and pay attention to the lecturer within you!!

This is key number one to true success, to a fulfilled life; to happiness... discovering your true self will make your life easier and more enjoyable.

How painful and difficult it is to cut down a tree with a knife – though it looks like the knife might actually get the tree down some day, the job is easier done with an axe because a knife was not built for cutting down trees. But this is how many people are living their lives, pursuing a life for which they were not built and armed, and therefore finding it so difficult.

Are you finding life difficult? Is what you are pursuing too hard for you? Are you enjoying your work or do you dread it the minute you think about it? Are you saddest on Mondays and happiest on Fridays? Perhaps you are a knife which is trying to cut down a forest and the project seems to never coming to an end!! Or maybe you are an axe but you are busy only cutting vegetables and you feel so dissatisfied because your full potential is locked up and unutilized.

Many from the adult population in formal employment, actually don't find fulfilment and satisfaction in their jobs; and because they have been locked up in the chase to make ends meet, they would not do anything about it apart from enduring the days, and for most, they find weekends as the only time they have to pursue their dreams, and their joy comes from what they do only in two days per week.
Under performance in jobs comes primarily from people that are misplaced and only work to earn a living; they work because they have to, not because they enjoy it.

True knowledge of one self, is the beginning of a purposeful and therefore meaningful and enjoyable lifestyle; and knowledge is truly more powerful than color.

Are you financially asleep or awake?

Chapter 2

You can MASTER anything you wish

Exploring your full self

*U*nlike what evolutionists would tell you, man was created very different from any animal you know.

Man is the only creature with the ability to create.

Man is the only creature with the ability to invent.

Man sits at the helm of all of God's creation. He is the only one that can tame another creature. No other creature can tame another creature let alone tame man.

Man is the only creature with creative abilities like that of God himself.

The material, with which man was made, has the ability to form a character that can master anything on this earth. In other words, man has the God material inside him.

Nothing is impossible to a dominion spirit, there are no limitations to a spirit of excellence; not even the sky can limit a soul that expresses its infinite potential.

There is a vast 'world' inside of man that is so big God himself can make a home inside.

"He has made every thing beautiful in his time: also he has set the world in their heart, so that no man can find out the work that God makes from the beginning to the end." Ecc 3.11

God, who fills the whole universe, can reside within one man. Just as man can hide in God, God also can hide in man; how big is man?
Am I implying that man is bigger than God? Obviously not, but am trying to explain a concept of man's limitless capacity built within his system. Physical dimensions cannot even begin to comprehend this concept.

The physical body around you is there to conserve physical space in the physical world.
If your body was as big as a house, your spirit and all your emotions will fill that body.
If your body was as big as the whole earth, your spirit will fill that body to capacity.

In other words, the spirit of a small man is not the same size as his body. How much you can achieve is not proportional to the stature of your body.

"You can do all things through Christ who gives you the strength…" Philippians 4:13

Your inabilities, your limitations and your failures are all due to the lack of true self perception. Your mastery and your achievements cannot be defined based on your physical status.
The expression of your true self is the key to mastery.
Every time the phrase *"I can't"* escapes your lips, you create a prison for your spirit and establish boundaries within which

you will operate. For instance, when you say "I can't swim", you send signals to your entire personality that trigger fear for water and cause your brain to operate within the spheres of this belief you have created for yourself. This limitation you have established for yourself will inhibit your spirit from releasing you towards the achievement of this goal.

I believe with all my heart that you can master anything you wish on this earth. You have abilities that no man can understand. You may not be a master of everything, but you can master anything.

The key to excellence is mastery. The only reason you are still an average person and getting average results, is that you have not applied the principles of mastery in your life.
It matters less who you are; the primary factor that determines your mastery is the environment in which you have been brought up. The environment you have chosen to create for yourself. No one race is above another race, no one color is above another color. Every person is a learning machine with abilities that can adapt to anything humanly possible.

The biggest contributor to your mastery but which can also be a very big obstacle is what we call culture. The culture of a people determines the general direction and future of those people. A working culture develops a prosperous people; a reading culture develops a knowledgeable people; an innovative culture develops a nation and an immoral culture develops a grave.

A normal human is by nature an imitator. From childhood, everything we learn is by imitation. A child learns to talk by repeating the words she hears from people around her. Your accent is also influenced by the people around you; people you talk with all the time. That is why it is easy to identify you by the way you speak; the Americans have an American accent, the British have a British accent, the Zambian man like me, has a Zambian accent; that's just the way it is; everyone comes from a certain culture and therefore bears a stamp or identity of that culture. Your culture or your environment also influences your beliefs. Many people are Christians because they grew up in a Christian environment; others are Moslems because they grew up there; a Hindu boy only knows Hindu values, so he grows up to be a Hindu. Your brain gets its orientation from the beliefs and values of your culture.

Therefore to develop an excellent spirit, the spirit of a master, you need to break records within your culture. You need to develop an independent culture; a culture that will allow you to attain mastery. The norm is to think and live within the confines of what you have been taught and what everyone believes.

Society embraces normal people and treats them respectably; it will give you a normal job and after you die offers you a normal burial and then forgets you ever existed. However, it is people who think outside the box who become masters; people who refuse to limit their minds within the cultures that reared them. These people can never be forgotten – people like Sir Isaac Newton, Albert Einstein and many others. History will never forget these people – it is impossible to forget masters. It is these people that contribute to the advancement of our society; people who many usually consider as lunatics.

A story is told of a group of such type of people many years ago; these people believed that they were capable of going to the moon – mind you this was before any attempts of going to the moon were made. They embarked on studies and experiments that would eventually land man on the moon and they referred to this as lunar explorations. The *normal* society thought these were insane, and mixing with them would make you equally insane. They coined a name for them and called them *lunatics or moon struck* – and that's where we get the word *lunatic* to literally mean someone who is insane, mad or foolish. Today, it is because of such people that man is able to go to the moon.

The greatest master that ever walked the face of the earth;

"*Ye call me Master and Lord: and ye say well; for so I am.*" John 13:13

His name was Jesus the Christ; he was the most independent of thinkers a man could ever meet. His peculiar way of thinking created a different culture for him that made people call him master when he was only 30 years old. Many people could not understand him in what he said and did so they ended up calling him demon possessed and insane; three years later he was put to death for claiming to be what they thought he wasn't and therefore accusing him of blasphemy. Two thousand years after his death, the world still calls him master.

No one person still affects the lives of such multitudes of people on earth than Jesus does today. Even our modern day calendar counts days after his birth; in other words, his birth is the reference point for our time.

True masters never die. *By the way Jesus rose from the dead.*

It is immoral to expect excellence from a person who has not attained mastery. Mediocrity in products and in services is due to lack of mastery. However, the world expects you to be a master of your business and skill and therefore expects only excellence.

The principles of Mastery

When I was younger, we liked watching kung-fu movies. Every weekend, there was what used to be called a martin show – specifically for younger audiences such as ours.
What I noticed in the kung-fu movies is that, there was always one person called *MASTER* otherwise also known as *TEACHER*. The most unfortunate part is that the master would always get killed somehow and then the main star of the movie would go on to avenge the death of his master. The point however, is that the master in the movie, was the man with the greatest skill of kung-fu; he was the teacher and role model of the main star in the movie.

The master did not become master by simply reading a kung-fu book. Today we have people with masters degrees all attained simply by reading books. A real master is one that can demonstrate his mastery.
To attain mastery, you must combine your theory with practice; you must perfect your theories by actually putting them to use.

The other thing I noticed in the kung-fu movies is that, the Master always had his own method of fighting; he had devised his own ways of always winning the fight. It was this skill that he would transfer into the main star of the movie.

A master always demonstrates his own peculiar method of achieving goals. A master is not a copy cat; a master develops the formula which others use to solve the equation.

The greatest obstacle to mastery is lack of focus. You cannot master multiple skills at the same time – and yet this is what we always see in many people. Ever heard the phrase:

"Jack of all trades and master of none?"

It is because the art of mastery requires being focused and persistent.

Remember, if you do not believe you can do it, you cannot do it. Choose to become a master at what you do; let your name be synonymous with your skill.

So, what really is the key to mastery?

(i) **M**ission

You cannot be a master and not know what your mission is. What do I mean here? Your mission is your reason, your purpose or your *why*. For centuries, the question of the meaning of life has rocked and thrown off-board countless numbers of people; the young and the old, the learned and the unlearned, the rich and the poor – and yet this alone remains the most important question every person on the planet must answer for themselves.

There must be some driving force that causes you to pursue a life of mastery without which you will have no reason to move from an average lifestyle. A clearly defined mission must be your blueprint in the development of a master in you.

What is it that you want to achieve at the end of it all? What is your goal and passion? It is dangerous to live life without a mission, without a purpose. Many people who end their lives after some frustration are people who never were passionate about anything. Many companies display on their walls what they call a mission statement. This document defines what the company wishes and plans to achieve in the market. It reminds them about their role and existence. This is a guideline which sets their boundaries of operation. Immediately a company forgets its mission statement, the competitor takes over.

You need to clearly define your goal which is your mission – what you want to become. Do not leave it to chance; and to always remind yourself about it, put it down on a piece of paper and frame it as your own mission statement, then hang it in your room so that your eyes will always look at it each time you wake up. The definition of your mission is the number one and most important step in the pursuance of your mastery.

(ii) **A**bilities

Each person is endowed with abilities to help them achieve their mission. You were uniquely framed and carefully packaged, ready to come and execute your mission on the planet. The abilities in you are what we sometimes call talents. You may have heard some people who are called multi-talented and others just talented. Well, the truth is that every person is multi-talented; you do not only have one ability in you!! There are inert multi abilities in you but you need to try them out to prove this. Other people are called disabled – this does not mean they are deprived of any abilities; NO ONE IS DISABLED. If one person does not have the ability you have, it does not mean they are disabled.

Ignorance is the only disability a man can successfully have;
And this is a disability of choice.

Let's take a blind man for instance who reads brail using his fingers, and a man who can see but can't read because he's never been in a classroom to learn how to read; who should we call disabled?

"The blind man because he can't use his eyes to read or the other man with eyes that can see but can't read?"

The truth is that these two people each have abilities except they are differently talented.
It is when you accept your condition of disability that you kill the genius inside you. Do not let anyone take advantage of you because your abilities are not their abilities.
Explore those hidden abilities in you that will help you achieve your mission statement.

You are disabled only if you choose to.

(iii) **S**elect
Even if you are endowed with many abilities, not all are there to help you achieve your mission. If your goal is to become the best saxophonist, your ability to translate Chinese may not be exactly the one you want to spend your time on. You need to carefully choose what you can improve on and can help you with your mission. You need to realize that all this goes back to achieving your mission – what and who you want to end up.

The point to note here is that, this venture is entirely your choice – you need to select. Just because you can sing does not mean you must end up a singer, but if you choose to, then the abilities in you that can make you the best singer are what you must select. You will not select to become everything because you cannot become everything. To become master, you must choose or select what you want to master or you'll end up Jack of all trades and master of none.

This is very critical because this is what makes people end up who they didn't intend to be. The abilities you choose to major on are what determine your destiny. You cannot choose one thing and end up another. If you are a swimmer and also a singer but you decide to always do your swimming – you will not be known as the best singer in town; most likely the title would be the best swimmer in town. So choose carefully your abilities.

A lot of people believe in what they call *fate*. They believe everything that happens to them was pre-ordained by the universe and everything they will ever experience is all an orchestration of this phenomenon called *fate*. I have such a great temptation to delve into this right now, but unfortunately, this is beyond the scope of this book; and all I can say here is that you have an undeniable and divinely instituted power of choice right in your hands. Which means that the world you will see tomorrow is equivalent to what you created today using your choices.

(iv) **T**raining
Once you have selected your abilities, you need to realize that you are not the best person that ever lived at your abilities or

talents; so you need to take them to the gym. Abilities are like babies, if you want them to grow and become perfect, you need to feed them and train them.

The best public speaker was not born like that, they took that gift to some bush and spoke to the trees; they spoke to anything and everything whether heard or not. They practiced the art until one day you saw the flare in their public speaking. But you think God somehow just blessed them with the gift and they had nothing to do with it.

Football legends don't fall from heaven, these are individuals who take their talents to the gym; even after training with their fellow team mates, and they take it a little further than everybody else.

Do not be cheated, no one is born with skill – this particular thing only comes after the gym.

Haven't you ever wondered why every man does not look like Rambo? Are you telling me some men don't have muscle? Everyone has muscle but it's the muscle that goes to the gym that shows.

(v) Explore

A master is not the person who only wins using one method. If your opponent steals your formula, what becomes of you? A master explores several ways of arriving at the same point. Explore your talents and discover several ways of scoring goals.

If you kick your penalties the same way, one day the goal-keepers will discover your method and that will be the end of your goal scoring carrier. How interesting it is to watch grand masters doing their thing. People are mesmerized by magic; they will pay you for the magic you put in your skill. Become an explorer of your own abilities and let people fight to get your auto-graph. No one will ever want your auto-graph until you become an explorer of your talents.

(vi) **R**inse & Repeat
There are no two ways about it and no short-cuts to mastery – if you want to master anything, doing it over and over, is the key. You cannot make piano master by playing one song per week; its repetition that does the job.

Back to my kung-fu movies analogy, I once watched a movie where a certain young monk wanted to learn kung-fu and he went to enroll at a monastery. His teacher's first lesson was that of discipline and commitment.
The young man was eager to learn so he thought this was good enough. His initial task was to sit by a river and slap the waters repeatedly with his palms. The first day he was all good, the second day came, the third came and went. He was looking forward to a time he would start learning kung-fu; a week past and he became inpatient. He approached his teacher rather furious and disappointed: "I came here to learn kung-fu, not to sit by the river slapping water like a fool!!" his teacher watched him and said "patience my child, patience".

Four months went by and it was time to go back on holiday to his family. By this stage he was so annoyed with the whole program he had made up his mind he was going to quit.
His family saw him coming home and they were all excited and happy to see their son and brother back obviously with some kung-fu skills to show off to them and his peers.
At the dinner table, his family decided to enquire from him what he had learnt at the monastery. Angrily, he replied

"I learnt literally nothing, am wasting my time there."

"hmm!!, am sure there is something you have picked up to show us!!" insisted his father.

"I don't want to go back to that place!!" he replied.

"Four months is a long time, you mean you were just sitting??" his mother added.

In anger, he slapped the dinner table from which they were eating - shouting *"I told you I learnt nothing!!"*
To the amazement of both his family and himself, the dinner table they once cherished broke into pieces after his one slap. It was then that he realized that the strength he had developed to break that strong table was as a result of those repeated slaps he was giving to that river of water.

To make master, you must overcome boredom that comes as a result of repetition. Even the bible says that:

"Now faith comes by hearing and hearing... " Romans 10:17

That is repetition right there; you need to keep hearing and hearing to get faith. It doesn't come because you heard it once last year – you must keep hearing it.

The six points to mastery spell out the word MASTER.
Mission, **A**bilities, **S**elect, **T**raining, **E**xplore and **R**epetition

Are you financially asleep or awake?

Chapter 3

If you do not sell anything, You will always be poor

Business is the ability to produce value that someone else needs

---

*Y*our entire life is a business entity, and the success of that business depends on how well you apply business management concepts in your own life. Each time you move out and open your mouth to speak, you are either increasing the value of that business or killing it.

From the book of beginnings, God gives us concepts which every business entity needs to thrive:

"...and God blessed them and said, be fruitful and multiply, replenish the earth and subdue it." Genesis: 1:28

The account above is when God created Mr. and Mrs. Adam; the first commandment and blessing they received from their maker was to be fruitful and to multiply; to replenish the earth, subdue and dominate it.

To be fruitful also means to be productive; to produce; simply put, to have a product. This command was given to man as it is also a requirement for every business entity.

There is no business without a product; otherwise what will you be selling? Every business must produce something. In the very same way, every person must produce something as an individual.

Jesus once said *"I am the vine and you are the branches... and every branch that bears no fruit will be cut down and thrown in the fire..."*

Productivity is essential, necessary and critical to your survival. You must produce. Not only were you commanded to produce, you were also blessed to produce; to bring forth from within you. This blessing and command does not only refer to producing children, which everyone has been glad to obey so far, but to also bring out other products which will be beneficial to people.

Secondly, man was commanded to *multiply* the product. Don't only produce one copy of your product and end there; reproduce that product. When a musician finishes his recording of an album, they make what is called a master copy. They do not end there; the next mission is to multiply that copy into millions of copies. When a writer publishes his book, he makes sure the copy is duplicated over and over and sometimes even into different languages.

When God made Adam, he never went back to make another Adam; he expected his product to replicate itself until the whole world was filled with replicas of Adam; the entire human race now is a multiplication of one Adam; even Eve came out of Adam.

Have you ever seen a Toyota corolla? Trust me; there are a million other Toyota corollas all over the world just like the one you saw. Toyota reproduced that one product; in other words they multiplied their product. What am I trying to communicate here?

Multiplication is a business concept on which businesses thrive. Produce your product and then multiply it by reproducing it all over again. Thirdly, man was commanded to *replenish* the earth. The word *"replenish"* also means to fill, to fulfil, to satisfy and to distribute.

The purpose of multiplying your product is to fill the market with it; to satisfy its demand on the market. In other words, you will need an effective distribution network for your product. Your product is meant to affect the different spheres of the world, not just your village.

Finally man was commanded to *subdue*. This word means to conquer and control. You are expected to conquer and control the market with your product and then you will have dominion.

Displaying your tomatoes at your market place is not the issue, the big picture is: is anyone buying your tomatoes? Is anyone interested in your product?

I once attended a sales presentation from a company that was closing deals like child play and I was wondering how in the world they managed to close so many big deals. They sure must have a vibrant sales team; they must be using some nice marketing phrases which no one else knows; they have the secrets of selling anything; and I was all excited about this meeting.

I was there in the presentation getting bored to the bone with this sales man reading some eligible words from some lousy

power-point which I thought *"anyone could do better with their eyes closed making that presentation!!"*
I thought to myself, they must have made a mistake; this guy is hardly putting any effort in selling this product!!

After the presentation, he faced the audience and mumbled a few words about payment terms.
A few minutes later, the prospecting customer handed over a hefty check to purchase the product.
What!!??, I exclaimed within myself. *"Something is not right!!"*
   "Sometimes it seems like the very best stuff sells itself!" I thought.

That's the key right there. This is what makes the difference between some dealers that have a waiting list and sell stuff for a premium while others look like ghost towns.
What matters more, is real marketing, marketing that involves making the right product, not hyping it. If your product is remarkable, it is also marketable.

Real business is business that invests in making remarkable products, products that are needed by prospects. If your prospects do not need your product, you will hardly sell anything. It's more like marketing yourself to an accounts firm with your civil engineering skills... they don't need civil engineers, they need accountants!!

Before you go out selling either your product or yourself, study your market first, and then brand your product to something your prospects can't refuse. This way, you won't go out hyping about your product. In other words, make a product that is capable of selling itself.

Whoever you are and wherever you are, we are all either

selling something or buying something. We are all in a buying and selling business; if you are not selling a product, you are selling yourself and if you are not buying a product or a service, you are buying someone. If you are doing none of these, you'll die hungry and very quickly; unless of course you are feeding from someone else actively involved in buying and selling; in which case you should ask yourself how long until you graduate from being a dependent.

The bible talks about the coming days of tribulation during which the anti-Christ will be in control of the entire economy and political status of the world.
This man will be so powerful that his word will be equivalent to law. He will cause everyone to bear his mark either on the forehead or on the palm of the hand. Everyone who refuses to bear the mark will not be able to *buy or sell* anything.
Why would the anti-Christ put such conditionality?
What is so important about buying and selling?

There will always be a market and there will always be consumers; you are a percentage of both and the variation of this percentage determines the level of your financial genius.

The key therefore, is putting value into a product that someone else needs; that is what is called business.
If you intend to sell yourself to a company as an employee, writing down mother Theresa's CV is not what will get you the job, if it does, they'll soon find out you are not mother Theresa after all. The secret is to brand yourself into a product that your prospect won't refuse; it's to make a product that delivers as much as it promises.

What are you selling? Is it needed by your buyers? What can

you do to increase its value? People want value for their money.

Answer these questions and put yourself on the road to building a successful business. Your life must be modeled as a business. Ask yourself how you can increase the value of the business of your life. Maybe you need to pick up some more skills in a particular area; or maybe you just need to sharpen some of your existing skills; whatever it is brand yourself as a remarkable product and go out and sell. Do not allow laziness and procrastination to trap you in mediocrity; you don't want to go out and buy a mediocre product, so why would you let yourself be a mediocre product and expect someone else to be thrilled with you?

The world only rewards excellence!! Any other reward is corruption!!

Are you financially asleep or awake?

Chapter 4

There's only one way to build wealth

Spend less than what you earn and invest the difference

*H*ave you ever heard of a phrase *"Money speaks"*? I once heard someone acknowledge the phrase and said "Y*es, I know money speaks, I heard it once, it said goodbye"*.

Money, in many people's hands, seems to have this common language and is always screaming *"spend me!!"* *"spend me!"* *"Spend me!"* And the screams sound so intimidating that many fail to hold it any longer.

When I started earning income years ago, I had a lot of needs to attend to that needed money to get resolved. Each month I'd get my pay check, it would all go to clearing my primary needs and each time I would always remain with nothing.

I always looked forward to a time when I would furnish my home completely and remain with extra monies to either save or invest in other ventures. However, the more pay-checks came to me, the more I saw the need to spend the money on very important things; and each time, I would promise myself to start my saving and investment plans the following month. Soon I was planning to get married and I had to spend even more towards this important occasion. I promised myself that as soon as I get married, then we can start investing the money towards our future and perhaps we can then become financially free so we can start pursuing our dreams.

Alas!! When my wife came home, the needs to warrant our expenditures doubled; a year passed by and as if that was not enough, our first baby was on its way – honey, you can't talk about investing now??? We need to plan for our baby…. And that's a whole lot of a project.

I soon realized that investing money, is a culture that you need to build and develop no matter how little or how much you earn.

I also learned another important lesson: 'needs never end'.

If you will wait until you meet all your needs before you can start investing your money, you might wait too long…

There is no magic in building wealth; your financial freedom is not a mystery or an accident, it's a formula whose only trick is to be committed to the plan and to doing it; and the principle behind this is simple 'spend less than what you earn, and invest the difference'. The key is to start NOW; the younger you are, the better; but even if you are old; as long as you know that your future is still coming, you need to prepare for it.

I have heard many people complain that they do not earn enough to even cover their basic needs, so how can they possibly even have something to invest or even save? It sounds very illogical. You could be in the same predicament.

Well, the truth is that, if today, you got an increment, there will most likely be no chance that you will meet all your needs; the most likely thing that will happen is that your needs will increase, you will unconsciously want to adjust your lifestyle to suit your increment; and with this adjustment comes new levels of spending. It is interesting to note however, that despite all your needs, and no matter how little your income seems to be, the government always gets their tax from it. If you looked at your pay slip and checked out the tax paid to date, you will realize that the government's faithfulness in removing from your pay check has really built a savings lesson for you. If you had been the one putting off that percentage into some savings, you certainly could have built a strong savings account.

Well, let's start putting down the strategy with some definitions and principles.

A normal working person considers his or her pay check as the only money classified as income. Therefore, if they get any monies other than from that pay check it is not income, and therefore is liable to any form of expenditure – after all, it is excess money.

This misconception is what causes most people to justify their spending habits and makes their stay in poverty an on-going story which never ends.

Now, redefining the meaning of *income:*
Income is any money that you earn by selling either your services or your products; this could come inform of a pay check from your job, or a pay check from your extra side jobs or private jobs. All this is classified as *income.*

Working from this principle, therefore, calculate how much income you earn per month and divide it in percentages to go in to various needs.

I will recommend the following practice to help you develop a culture of saving and investing your money no matter how little or how much you earn.

Your total income is pegged at 100%, and beginning from there, we will apportion this income in percentages:

(a) *10% Tithing*

The principle of giving and receiving is one that works irrespective of who is practicing it; it's a principle and therefore works for anyone. One would argue this and think otherwise. The most human thing to do when you think you have little money in your hands is to hold on to it and not give some away but rather spend it on yourself. This is the thinking of people or nations which will remain poor.

"There is that scatters and yet increases, and there is that withholds more than is necessary, but it tends to poverty." Proverbs 11:24

The principle of giving works on anything you decide to give: in other words, if you want something, you must give that thing away. If you want a smile, you must give one first and a smile will come back to you. You can't be praying for a smile and yet looking at me with a frown!! That prayer just won't be answered!! If you want blows on your face, walk to the street and punch someone on their face, I assure you, you'll get blows on your face; this is when "give and it shall be given back to you" really works very quickly. Now, this might sound funny, but it is working on the same principle; if you want money, give money.

I realize, it's not easy to just part away with monies like that if you have not developed the character of giving. You do not necessarily have to start with 10% to give; however, if it's a *tithe,* it can't be anything other than 10% because the word tithe literally means tenth. You can start with whatever is comfortable with you, but the idea is you must start to give… this will help you to develop the character of giving which is essential for enabling you to start *saving and investing.*

If you cannot give, it's practically impossible for you to save or invest your money; because investing is just like giving away — it's letting go, deferring the pleasures of spending it now.

(b) *15% Towards investments*

Have you ever heard the phrase *"Pay yourself first"*? a money making principle from Napoleon Hill from his popular book *Think and Grow Rich.* what this means is: before you look at all your bills and all the expenses on your plate, remove a percentage from your income (more like the tax man does it) and pay yourself first. Now, this does not mean that you should slice a chunk from your income and go and party with it; this money goes straight to your investment basket. After this, then look at your other expenses and let them come secondary.

Again, you do not necessarily need to follow these figures religiously; start with whatever percentage is comfortable with you. The idea is for you to start.

The biggest question though, for so many is: what can I invest in? Others always have the excuse that *"my money is too little to invest in anything"*. Well, to begin with, if it was too little to invest in anything, then is also not too little for you to even use for anything? would you then consider putting it away in some savings account since it's too little for you to use now? some people teach that saving small amounts is a waste of time, so you will spend it?

What I have found out is; although people would tell you that the money is too little, they will still find a way of spending that little money and therefore not give it a chance of ever growing;
(it's more like eating little chickens before they mature).
Investing is a game, and the less you play, the little you know about how to...
Many people think that the word *"invest"* is a special reserved word for the rich; and therefore it can only be spoken and understood by the rich.
Tables have been turned upside down; you do not invest because you are rich, but rather, you become rich because you invest.

There are so many investment options in the market and it really all goes with your emotions, your likes, your dislikes and so on. Some may find it interesting and easy to invest in real estate, while others will find it too boring and difficult but would rather play with stocks, mutual funds, government bonds, treasury bills, unit trusts and the like; others would just do well at trading, buying and reselling items for profit. The principle thing is; find what you like, get some information of how you can effectively and rationally get into that market, and then begin putting your money there. It does not make sense to throw your money into some investment you are not familiar with.
The keyword is: get the knowledge and start investing your

money NOW.

(c) *15% Savings*

Whenever, you don't feel safe about putting your money into some investment, put it in your savings but never defer paying yourself first to other expenses. However, aside from having investment instruments, you also need a separate savings basket where you will consistently be putting away a certain percentage of your income. This is not a pension scheme. Pension schemes came in and are mandatory for most because many people are naturally not savers; so they are forced to be part of some pension scheme to allow them save something for their retirement income.

The savings we are referring to here is something apart from your pension scheme.

I had a colleague who shared with me, that he had tried to save but each time, he found himself going back into his savings and eating from it, and was wondering how best to achieve a consistent savings plan..

> *It has been said that: if you cannot save anything from your income, the seeds of greatness are not in you*

Most people try to save without defining the reason for the particular saving and therefore do not see the need of not actually spending that money now. There are various reasons you want to save money; it is not just for the sake of stacking up some cash somewhere. Some of the reasons would be; to save for some rainy days: eventualities happen unexpectedly and most times, at times when you are not ready to handle them; you don't want to be caught unawares and panic through the events. Other reasons would be to save for your kids' education or to buy a new car. This type is a long term type of saving where you need to lockup the money into some deposit account that allows you only to withdraw the monies after a certain period.

There are several other reasons you want to have a savings basket, but for whatever reason, you need to have this savings basket. If however, you do not define a reason for your savings, it may be tempting to jump back into your basket for any petty reason and begin eating from your savings. The important thing is: define the reason, put rules to your account and abide by them.

(d) 60% Remaining goes to your daily running costs

You cannot afford to have 100% of your income all go to your running costs.
Most families use all their income into their running costs and justify it by claiming they cannot afford to take any part of it elsewhere. Your income must dictate your lifestyle and determine your means. In other words, if your expenditure is more than your income, you are living beyond your means and must consider adjusting your lifestyle or look for more sources of income to support that lifestyle. There is no need to be in competition with your neighbors or friends because their goals may not necessarily be your goals.

If your expenditure is always going beyond your income, you need to re-examine your expenses.
Perhaps your rental costs are too high, or your mortgage repayment was not thought through conclusively and has sky-rocketed your expenses, or your shopping list contains unnecessary toys, or your loan went into purchasing a liability

and now the repayment is hurting you. Whatever it is, you need to sit and re-examine your expenses and adjust where possible.

If you find that you are living beyond what you can financially bear, begin to adjust slowly while also looking for other sources of income.

Building wealth is a skill, and it does not happen overnight, it requires consistence, persistence and a lot of commitment. All these characteristics result from a thought pattern contrary to a spender's thought pattern. Anyone, no matter who they are or where they are, can build wealth for themselves. It is not about how much you earn, but what you do with what you earn, no matter how little it appears to be.

Most rich people didn't start with fat salaries and hefty benefits; they were only committed to their dream and persisted for many years.
They always believed they were rich way before the first penny ever touched their pockets.

My recommendations and suggestions here may sound like am advocating that you should live below your means; which is completely contrary to what I am trying to communicate.
I have seen and met some so called "rich" people who hardly spend any of their pennies; they drive 1980 models, they dress like Lazarus, eat beggars for lunch and go to the cheapest hospitals whenever they require medical attention.
What is the use of wealth if you are mesmerized by a poor man's lifestyle?

I have also met people who are barely making it but want to

live like Rose Perot – they spend before they earn just to keep up appearances.

Both of these two types of people are living in the two extremes of life. A person needs to live in the middle of the road or they will fall into the ditch on either extreme sides of the road.

What I mean is; you need to be balanced. Live within what you can afford and if what you want is beyond your means, then find ways of expanding your means. Don't go out and borrow just to satisfy your wants.

I have also met a lot of people who do not want to have anything to do with money and wealth; to them just mare discussion or even reading about money is an unpardonable sin. One thing I can say to you is this; God is the one who gives you power to create this same wealth – so go right ahead and create it if you can!!

Are you financially asleep or awake?

Chapter 5

What's the use of being Debt free and yet broke?

How to handle debt

*T*he sound of the word debt sends shivers into most people's spines and they never want to go that direction while others find debt as an every day companion. Many have a notion that debt is bad and so must be avoided at all costs. We have organizations lobbing for debt cancellations for individuals and nations in the hope that after their debt has been cleared then they can pavement their way to prosperity.

If you as an individual or a nation gets into so much debt that you see cancellation as your only hope of the way out, then your financial intelligence needs some tweaking.

Because of the effects of bad debt on many people and nations, there is a widespread misconception that debt is bad, and yet many rich people use debt to build their wealth.
Debt has the ability to make you very rich but it also has the ability to make you very poor and bankrupt.

There are two types of debt: there is good debt and there

is bad debt. Good debt is good, and bad debt is bad. It sounds so basic, but that's just it.

What is bad debt?

It is the beginning of the year, and you just came out of a festive period where you spent most of your income on goodies and merry making. The month is long before your next income, but you need to settle your bills, your rentals are due, your kids need to go back to school, the utility company is calling you every day and you only have one option of getting a loan from some financial institution that is lending out at a humongous interest rate. You go ahead and get the loan to service all these bills and now you are committed to paying it back for a whole year.

Debt that falls within these confines is termed as *bad debt*. It is called bad debt because you will need to personally service it from your income. So instead of apportioning a percentage of your income towards some savings or investments, you will now be required to do that to service this debt. This is the kind of debt that prevents you from building wealth for yourself. It is bad debt.

Any debt you incur that goes towards servicing of a liability is a bad debt, and you should avoid such debts at all costs. Hmm "Liability"? that's a big word!! Well it simply means getting a loan to go and pay rent, pay school fees, buy a car, do house shopping or indeed service another loan. This type of debt is not the kind that makes you rich; this kind creates more poverty for you.

On the other hand, there is what is also called *good debt*.

What is good debt?

For many years, the rich have used the advantage of good debt to build wealth for themselves. To begin with, if you are going to acquire any debt at all, it MUST be for the purposes of acquiring an asset, not a liability. Oops, another big word "asset".

The word Asset means a lot of different things to different people and if you really want to confuse yourself even further about it, no offences intended here, but go ahead and ask an accountant what the word means.

Let's be as simple as we can be and say; an asset is anything that pays me, while a liability is anything I have to pay.

So if you list down everything and everyone you have to pay, that's your liability list; and if you list everything and everyone that pays you, that's your asset list.

Many people have only one item in their asset list; their job, and a very long list of items on their liability list. Just looking at these two lists can quickly tell you whether you are headed for hail or for wealth.

Okay, let's get back to what is good debt. With our little description above, we can therefore safely say that good debt is debt used to acquire an asset, something that will be paying you. So if you go out and get a loan to buy a car, or pay rent or furnish your home, ask yourself this question: are you buying an asset or are you buying a liability? It is not wise to get a liability only to go and buy another liability; this increases items on your liability list and this does not produce wealth but poverty.

When you acquire debt, for example a loan, you need to structure your repayment strategy so that you will not require repaying the debt from your current income, but from what your asset will be producing for you. Or, you should plan it in such a way that, even if you pay it back from your income, the returns from your asset will cover all your incurred costs from the debt.

Now, there are different assets and we will not go into that now, but as a rough guide, if you are blank about what assets to buy, the first asset you should buy is your financial education.
It is therefore, not clever to only work towards being debt free, and yet remain so broke. You need to be debt free from all bad debts – debt that you acquire from shopping dollies is all bad debts. Avoid it all if you can.

Do not be afraid of good debt; go out and look for some good deals and when you have structured your deal with a win-win approach, find some money and begin building your wealth using other people's money.

Building your wealth through good debt is what rich people call *building wealth using other people's money*; that's why they say it doesn't take money to make money – and everybody else thinks *"I need money to make more money"*.

If you want to live an average lifestyle with only enough to go by, avoid all types of debt – live within what you earn and play it safe. But if you want to be wealthy, learn how to acquire good debt.

Are you financially asleep or awake?

Chapter 6

Repent, for the kingdom of Heaven has arrived

*Change your thinking to one that supports
a healthy & wealthy lifestyle*

What first comes into your mind when you hear the word "repent"? I can bet there is no evangelist or preacher who has never used this word; in our context, it has come to mean: to turn away from sin; to turn to God; to forsake the old ways of life and embrace the new life of righteousness in Christ Jesus.

When Jesus begun his preaching ministry, he had only one message; "The kingdom of God"; and whenever he opened his mouth to teach, he would always say: "And the kingdom of God is like unto …".

He was introducing a new concept which before, had never been taught and heard this way. The people's training and belief in that time, was based on the Jewish teachings taught by the rabbis in the synagogues.

Jesus' first message was "Repent for the kingdom of heaven has arrived"

"From that time Jesus began to preach, and to say, Repent: for the kingdom of heaven is at hand." Mat 4:17

The word 'Repent' in the passage above has nothing to do with turning away from sin per say.

The word *'Repent'* in the passage above has nothing to do with turning away from sin per say. The literal meaning of the word is *"to think differently"*; it is to change your way of thinking; to experience a paradigm shift in your mind.

In other words, Jesus was literary saying: "change the way you think!! Put on a different culture!! If you are in Judaism, stop thinking Judaism; if you are a Muslim, stop thinking like a Muslim, if you are a Christian, stop thinking like a Christian – *change the way you think."*

Why would Jesus begin his preaching ministry this way?

Until then, no one had talked about the kingdom of God in the way that Jesus taught. No one knew how to live in the kingdom. The kingdom of God is not like the kingdoms of this world; your government is not exactly a replica of the government of God; to live in the kingdom of God, you need to destroy (literally put off) the concepts and ideologies you learned from the worldly systems that war against the concepts and ideologies of the kingdom of God, and you need to pick on the new concepts of the kingdom of God; now to do this, you need to completely change the way you think – in other words, you need to *repent.*

The kingdom of God is about peace, love and joy; and this is not so in the worldly governments and kingdoms.

To move from sadness to happiness, something must happen in your mind.

To move from sickness to health, something must happen in your mind.

To move from poverty to wealth, something must happen in

your mind. To move from death to life, something must happen in your mind. Jesus knew exactly how critical it was to first deal with the state of the mind of a person to get them to cross over to the other side.

What Jesus was saying is: *"I have come to introduce you to a new kingdom; a kingdom of peace, love and joy; a kingdom of abundant life. You don't have to continue carrying your heavy burdens; put them down and carry mine which is easy and light".*

Jesus was saying *"I need to recruit citizens, but these citizens must think like citizens of this kingdom and it's different from the way you currently think, therefore, change the way you think!"* In other words, repent"

How should your thinking be then?

Your thinking should be one that always puts you above circumstances; one that makes you a conqueror. Your thinking should not be of fear and failure but of faith and success.

Through out the word of God, the bible, you hear words like:

You are more than a conqueror.
You are a mighty man of valor.
You are well able and you will overcome.
Greater is He inside you than he that is in the world.
There are more who are with you than against you.
No weapon formed against you will prosper.
You will tread upon scorpions and serpents.

All this, is to make you adopt a successful man's mind-set. Even doctors have confirmed that it is much easier to treat and bring to life a patient with a mind-set of faith and success than the fearful and terrified.

When the Israelites were in the wilderness and twelve spies

were sent to go and spy on the land of promise, only two came back with a positive and hopeful report and were confident that they would possess the land. The other ten were full of fear and fright. The ten spies died in the wilderness from natural causes; the two who were positive and confident, made it to the Promised Land.

It is not magic nor witchcraft, neither is it bad luck – your survival is dependent on your mind-set. This is why Jesus had to deal with the issues of the mind first; change your thinking.

If you can change the mind of a man, you have won the man. We live in a world today, where the word *terrorism* has entered our vocabulary with so much force and has brought a lot of instability and fear in many lives. The so called terrorists have a certain mind-set trained to completely believe that their actions are endorsed by the almighty God; and when they blow themselves up together with innocent lives they consider as infidels, they see this as the highest form of martyrdom and await the greatest reward from their god in paradise.

You cannot stop such a person by force. A man who is willing to die for his cause needs only a confrontation with his mind – no amount of force will stop this man; you can arrest his body, but if you have not arrested his mind, you have not solved the problem; you cannot destroy a man's belief system using guns and grenades.

"Come now, and let us reason together, says the LORD: though your sins be as scarlet, they shall be as white as snow; though they be red like crimson, they shall be as wool." Isaiah 1:18

A man without God is a terrorist to his own soul; and to save him from his own terrorism, God begins by appealing to his reasoning, which is his mind; "come let us reason together…."

The scripture quoted above is God's direct confrontation with man's mind to make him change and take a different turn of life.

There are more people imprisoned in their minds than what we have in our physical prisons.

In the bible, during the time of Joshua after Moses' time, God instructed Joshua to go and drive out the people from the land that God promised the Israelites; and they were to possess it as their own. Joshua's instruction was to utterly destroy and kill; and he carried out the orders to the letter; he wiped the land clean from the infidels that dwelt there. No one was considered innocent, not the children and not the women or the animals; they all received the same fate.

I would like you to think for a moment about the similarities between the Joshua of the bible and the modern day terrorist.

Joshua believed in God.
The terrorist believes in some God.
Joshua believed he was under instruction from God.
The terrorist believes he is under instruction from some God.
Joshua believed that carrying out these orders to the letter was his highest duty.
The terrorist believes that carrying out his attacks to the letter is his highest duty.
Joshua believed that killing the infidels was doing God's

work. The terrorist believes killing the people he thinks are infidels is doing God's work.
Joshua held no one as innocent.
The terrorist thinks no one is innocent.

The terrorist is not fighting a war because he needs justice for the injustices he has suffered. The terrorist is fighting because he believes he fulfils God's purpose when he does this. His mind believes so much that what he does is the will of God. Coming against the terrorist with force is like coming against Joshua's army with force. A confrontation with the mind is the war you need to engage with the person whose beliefs are contrary to yours.

What has all this got to do with being financially Awake?

What you believe in your mind, is what you will become in your life.
To become a millionaire, you need to adopt the mind-set of a millionaire.
To become a success, you need the mind-set of a successful man. To become a terrorist, you need to adopt the mind-set of a terrorist. As a man thinks in his heart (mind), so is he.

That is why the bible says:

"Keep your heart (mind) with all diligence, for out of it are the issues of life." Proverbs 4:23

When the bible here makes reference to the word *heart,* this is not pointing to the organ that pumps blood in your body; this is referring to your mind which is responsible for controlling your entire personality. In other words, your *heart* out of it, are the issues of life. The word used to *'keep'* is also translated *'to guard'* or *'to protect'* or 'to *secure'* or 'to *watch over'*. A paraphrase of the script therefore would be:

Guard your mind, protect your mind, secure your mind and watch over your mind, for out of it, are the issues of life.

The mind is a very important part of your being. Pay attention to what goes into your mind. Because once your mind learns what you have given it to learn, it's not easy to make it unlearn. To simplify this even further; consider whatyou read, what you hear and what you see, because all these become part of your mind from where your life springs.

It's your choice; the one thing that you have total control over, is the mind and the way you think. No one person can imprison your mind and choose your thoughts; this is a realm which only you can control, not even God can choose the way you think – you have the power to choose your thoughts, therefore, repent and choose a thought pattern that will support a healthy and wealthy lifestyle. Your mind is the factory from which your destiny is manufactured. What you think, is what you end up.

Are you financially asleep or awake?

Chapter 6

You were wired for the TOP

A normal person does not enjoy poverty,
sickness and disease

There's no normal person who enjoys poverty and wants to continue in it. A normal person does not celebrate pain and desire to continue this way. There's no normal person who always wants and enjoys being below other people.

"Under circumstances" and "under the weather" are not the best responses anybody wishes to give after a friendly greeting.

Everyone dreams of being great, powerful, healthy and wealthy even if it may never happen. You were made this way, to always better your life. The TOP was your original position.

Your system was never designed to live and enjoy pain; to live below your capacity; that is why whenever a foreign object introduces pain, sickness and disease in your system, your body, without your consent, immediately begins to react and fight back. When there's an infection in your body, your doctor will normally check your blood to see the percentage of your white blood cells; when there is a higher presence of these cells in your blood, the doctor immediately knows that your blood has been infected. The body produces extra white blood cells – these are soldier cells that fight infections in your blood. This happens because, your body was never wired to accept and live in sickness; otherwise it would allow

56

sickness with no interjections. Your body was created to self-heal. Have you ever wondered why if you are broke and have bills as high as Mount Kilimanjaro, you are not at the best of your moods?

Your system was not just wired for such circumstances.

There is an emotional and biological mechanism built inside you to soldier against any foreign intrusions that introduce any situation that otherwise place you below the TOP. Religion wants you to accept your condition whatever it is (poverty, sickness, disease, pain etc) as the will of God. Religion says, if it's God's will, you will be healed; the bible says, you were healed when Jesus hung on the cross; religion says, if it's God's will, you will prosper; the bible says he became poor so you can become rich; religion says if it's God's will, that pain will go away; if it's God's will, you will make it through. But for so many people, it never seems to be God's will…

Many who believe that God is teaching them something through their sickness, still go to hospital to make sure they get well – seems to me like they are fighting against God's will.

Others who think poverty is a sign of holiness and humility, still wake up every morning to go and work for money.

Poverty has no relationship to holiness any more than you are related to baboons, or is it homo-habilis as school history would have you believe. Poverty is not a sign of holiness neither is it a sign of how close you are to God; if it were, many people in Africa, India and the like would be the holiest bunch of people on the face of the earth today.

As a matter of fact, the very God we think delights in our

poverty stricken selves, apparently lives in a place glamorously adorned with streets of pure gold, the gate leading to his throne has all the most precious of stones your eye has never seen.

Just the description of the dwelling place of God himself, gives you an idea that you are not dealing with a broke God. How unfair therefore, can he be to only delight himself with us in our poorest of states? Everyone who believes in God, wants to go to heaven where God is, why? If heaven was full of worms and smells like that smell you don't like; if the streets were made of charcoal and poverty was the order of the day… I assure you, not many would want to go to heaven. The reason for this is that you were not wired to delight in poverty, pain and suffering – in other words, you don't want hell.

This is what I call an involuntary *knee jerk* against poverty, pain and suffering.

Your potential is expressed to its maximum when all the necessary resources for its operation are in place – and brother, that takes money this side of heaven. No matter how brain washed you get about not living at the top, everything within you screams out that you were not just wired for the dungeon.

I have heard a lot of stories about people who escaped from somewhere – none of those places they escaped from were a palace full of goodies and juices; they all escaped either from prison, death, or some tragic situation. No one wants to escape from a good life; everyone gravitates towards goodies.

To me, the word TOP really stands for "Taking Original Position". Until you are back to where you belong, you have not started living a normal life. When you take back your original position, you have truly repented and have regained your life back.

The top is a place of kingship and control; it's a place of leadership and responsibility. The top is a place for masters, not for slaves and subjects. The top is where you belong – but you cannot belong to the top simply by stating that you belong there. When Mr. and Mrs. Adam fell from the top, it ceased to be your birthright to belong to the top. You now need to apply some effort to get back to your original position.

I wish I could tell you that your way back to your original position is in three easy steps; but unfortunately, it's a journey that involves the entire process called *REPENT*. The word "REPENT" is a combination of two words "Re" and "Pent". "Pent" means TOP and "Re' means *to take back*. Therefore, to *repent* is to be taken back to the top. But the process of being taken back to the top is a process that involves reprogramming and re-engineering the way you think; because the literal meaning of the word *Repent* is *to think differently*.

It is impossible to live in total health when your thinking tells you that sickness is normal.

It is impossible to live in wealth when your thinking tells you that poverty is normal.

It is impossible to live in abundance if your mind is wanting.

If you know you belong to the top, begin a mind reprogramming process that will take you back to your original position.

You belong to the TOP.

Are you financially asleep or awake?

Chapter 7

Your future is not in God's hands – it's in yours

Putting responsibility back in your hands

$\mathcal{A}$ quick glance at the statement above may cause some to label me a heretic. For so long, we have been taught not to worry about tomorrow for tomorrow will worry about itself. Unfortunately, to so many the phrase: 'to worry' means exactly like the phrase 'to plan'.

'Do not worry about tomorrow' does not mean ignore tomorrow and let it just roll without your plans.

Many years ago, as the story goes, there lived a wise old man in a village. His name was called *The Oracle*. The Oracle's wisdom in dealing with community issues made him very respectable and revered by all the people that lived there. They called him the Oracle because he never minced his words when it came to advice and dispute management. His reputation was such that he had never failed to handle any issue in the community and hence all the villagers regarded him as the mentor of their time.

One day, two young boys set out on a mission to trick this old man so he could fail to solve their problem and for the very first time, his reputation would change and people would never again regard him as their mentor.

So the boys caught a little bird and planned that they'd go to the Oracle and hiding the bird in their hands, would ask the Oracle whether the bird was alive or dead. If the Oracle says the bird is alive, then the boy holding it behind, would squeeze it until it dies; if however , the Oracle says the bird is dead the boy would then keep the bird alive; and the Oracle for the first time would fail and look foolish to the entire village.

So the boys started off for their little scheme and arrived at where the Oracle used to live.

'*Mr. Oracle*' they called, '*we have a little problem and we were wondering if you could help us solve it!*'
'*What's the matter little friends?*' asked the Oracle.
'*In our hands is a little bird,*' they said
'*We want you to tell us if the bird is alive or dead*'

The Oracle looked at the boys and smiled. Then he said some of the most remarkable words that can forever change your history.

'*My little friends,*' he replied,
'*Whether that bird in your hands is alive or dead, is entirely up to you*'.

The little story above may not be biblical, but explains graphically the power of choice in our hands. Everything you were meant to become, you can become. Notice here that I didn't say I you will become.

As far as God is concerned, your future, your greatness and your wealth is certain, but whether you will reach there, is entirely up to you.

"Many are the PLANS in a man's heart, but the LORD will give direction to the path." Proverbs 16:1

It is amazing how many people just allow life to take them wherever it's going. Their lives are full of surprises because they never plan for anything at all, and when they die, their death is always untimely and premature.

There is a difference between worrying and planning. When you worry about what you will eat or wear, you are not solving a problem, you are just creating another problem to rally alongside an already existing one.

When you plan what you shall eat or wear, God feels good, because you have just given him what to do. He says *'commit all your plans (NOT WORRIES) to him, and he'll determine the course of action.'* In other words, he will execute the plans committed to him.

God will never plan for your life – he expects you to do the planning and let him worry about bringing it to pass.

You might say, but the scripture says God has plans for me!!...

"For I know the plans I have for you, says the LORD, good plans not bad plans, plans to give you an expected end." Jeremiah 29:11

God only has one plan for you – to give you an expected end. In other words, what you expect, God is committed to make it come to pass. In short, if you expect nothing, nothing is what you will get; otherwise, no one would be a failure.

One of my favorite preachers Dr. David Oyedepo says:

"Expectation is God's wisdom for His manifestations"

What you choose today, determines what you'll become tomorrow. If you choose nothing, you'll become nothing. God may have intended for you to become the president of your country, but the ultimate choice of becoming the president lies in your hands. Whether that bird is alive or not, is entirely up to you. Your future is written in your own handwriting.

Not every seed will become a tree, but every seed can become a tree. The question is: which seed are you? The one that rots and never makes it or the one that is planted and finally becomes the tree that it was always meant to be? Your future is in your hands.

Have you ever heard of palm readers? these con men whose job is to look at your hands and from there derive what is supposedly to be your future.

so they'll read your palms and tell you what you should expect tomorrow.

These people are diviners and they play with familiar spirits, so I don't recommend this venture as the way to know your future.

"A man or woman who calls upon spirits or fortune-tellers or magicians shall be put to death by stoning; their blood is upon them... anyone who turns to mediums and fortune-tellers or magicians prostitutes himself by following them, I will set my face against him, and will cut him off from the people"
Leviticus 20: 6, 27

These fortune tellers are right about one thing though; they are reading from your hands; what they should in fact be telling you is that your future is right there in your hands – go read it yourself.

Someone said: *The quickest way to predict the future, is by inventing it* – use your hands and invent the future you want to see; if you don't, you will still have a future, except it won't be too different from yesterday; how boring, it's like playing a broken record; in short your past will keep repeating itself.

"*And say to Archippus, Take heed to the ministry which thou hast received in the Lord, that thou fulfil it.*" Col 4:17

Paul the apostle of Jesus Christ was concluding his letter to the Christians at Colosse called the Colossians. During his final salutations and instructions, he says these important words:

Say to Archippus, take heed to the ministry which you received in the Lord, that you fulfil it.

The word *"ministry"* also means "work" or "service"; in other words, your ministry is your work; it is also your purpose for existence. This does not refer to preachers only; everyone has a ministry.
The ministry of a preacher is to preach the word of God.
The ministry of a doctor is to minister healing to the sick.
The ministry of an engineer is to minister engineering concepts to his products.
The ministry of a lawyer is to offer attorney services to his clients.

Now, the words of Paul suggest that the fulfilment of Archippus' ministry (purpose) is dependent on Archippus himself. If Archippus does not take heed to his ministry, his ministry will suffer. Therefore, the fulfilment of your purpose in life is dependent on you and you alone.

If you do not manage to fulfil your purpose in life, be ready to take the blame for it. Your future is in your hands.

Are you financially asleep or awake?

Chapter 8

The real purpose of money

So you can have fewer questions in life, for money "answereth" all things

---

When man fell from being a dominion spirit to being a slave of sin, suddenly, he had so many questions with very few answers. The most tragic thing is that, over the decades, man's relegation to being a slave of sin also made him acquire another secondary master called money. This master called money has gained so much popularity that the entire world now works and slaves for him. Kings and their subjects both bow to the master called money.

God himself also acknowledges the great influence that this master has on earth and recognizes him as the only true rival to himself:

"No man can serve two masters: for either he will hate the one, and love the other; or else he will hold to the one, and despise the other. Ye cannot serve God and money." Mat 6:24

Apparently, God makes no mention of the devil in this passage; he considers the devil of no match to him compared to the rivalry from money. In other words, money is more powerful than the devil. That is why the devil has used money to propagate his evil acts.

Over 90% of all crimes are money related. Think about the killings, the drugs, the prostitution, and the robberies. Most divorces are as a result of financial problems and misunderstandings.

All these are manifestations of the leadership of money under the control of the devil. Understanding the purpose of money is one of the most important keys to your freedom and to the fulfilment of your God given dreams.

The passion that motivated God to creating man was so that man could master His creation. God wanted to extend His influence to earth through the man He created. However, as the story goes, man got corrupted and could no longer fulfil God's original intention. But this did not kill the passion in God's heart. God was willing to do anything, even to become man and die (Since God cannot die), to just make sure man succeeded in what was originally intended for him – to be master on earth.

When man was relegated from his authority, Lucifer assumed the position and became the god of this world instead of man. However, Lucifer the devil, quickly saw that he was unfit to master man and he therefore needed an ally to successfully control man forever – unfortunately, he found this ally in money; and has, since then, used money to frustrate the plans of God on earth.

Money does not have any authority of its own except the authority you give it. Lack of understanding of the purpose of money can forever keep you a slave of money. In other words, money can only assume the power that you give it. It was this same power of money that was used to betray the son of God for the crucifixion.

To fully understand the purpose of money, we need to address what it is not intended for:

1. Money is not for making you happy

If you are an unhappy person, more money will not make you happy.
If you are a stingy person, more money will not make you generous. This is a false front that money has created to millions of people. They think, if they could just have a million dollars, they'd be the happiest people on earth – so they work and work harder for the master. The greater this illusion becomes, the more one is likely to fall into the crimes of money.

Most of those robbers and bandits are the saddest people living on earth today, and they genuinely need help. Most of them think happiness will come from acquiring money – and by whatever means they use, they go for it, just to be happy.
Money tends to amplify your personality. If you are a happy person, more money will make you share your happiness more. If you are a generous person, more money will amplify your generosity. If you are a sadist on the other hand, more money will only create a myriad of enemies for you.

2. Money is not for making you rich and famous

This sounds so contradictory and ambiguous, but it has been an illusion passed on from generation to generation.
Always remember this:

You are not poor because you do not have money – you do not have money because you are poor.

The issue has been turned the other way round. It is not that if you have money, you'll be rich and famous (you may), but

If you are rich and famous, you will have money. Man has this great inert need in him for fame – this is so because, remember he was created to be a king, but now he is a slave, but still has those desires of a king in him; and because he does not know how to break away from slavery, he tries to get fame illegally and falls in a trap.

If you had all the money to do anything you ever wanted to do, what would you be doing? Would you still be waking up every morning to go to that job you go to everyday? Would you still want to go to school and further your education?

If you still cannot figure out what you would be doing if you had all the money, then you have not found your purpose in life and everything you are doing now, is just a chase after money.

Money is not an end, but a means to the expression of your full potential. It's meant to be a resource, not a master –

3. *Money is not for controlling other people.*

Some people have a witches' mentality. They love to control other people; they love to master and to lord over other people – they are big bullies.

Even if man was created to control earth, he was not created to control fellow humans; his authority was to tame animals, not fellow humans.

Controlling people is not the reason for money, this is how the devil uses money; to control humans – and he is the chief of all witches, therefore, using money this way, only makes you Lucifer's ally.

The number one reason for money

Money is the most treasured resource to help you get the

freedom and ability to explore your destiny. The bible says that money is an answer to questions. Money is there to help you become all you can become and to help you cause others to become all they can become. For many if not all, the main obstacle to living their dreams and fulfilling their purpose in life is merely lack of time on their hands; the little time they seem to have is all spent looking or working for money.

Imagine if you had all the money you ever needed to do money is your tool not your boss. Money will cause you to touch the people you cannot touch without it. It will unfold possibilities you thought were not possible. It causes you to be empowered and to empower others. Millions die of hunger, but money has the ability to answer this question.

The ability of money to answer questions, depends in whose hands it is in, money has no power of its own.

Go sell and give to the poor

One day a rich young ruler approached Jesus and asked him a question about how he could enter heaven. The young man had kept all the commandments but money still had a grip on him; he was a ruler but not of money, money was still ruling him. Jesus perceived this, and instructed the fellow to go and sell his belongings, give to the poor, and then come follow Jesus.

Now, it is very easy to misunderstand scripture, and develop a doctrine around some recorded event in the bible. Some people think, to follow Jesus, you must sell what you have, give to the poor, remain broke and then follow him.

Have you ever wondered why emphasis has been placed on

taking the gospel to the poor? The poor do not need money to get them out of poverty, they need the gospel; but what is the gospel?

The gospel is knowledge of the principles of the kingdom of God, which is good news to the poor. It is good news because it shows them how to escape from poverty, how to put meaning to life and how to run after their God given dreams. The poor do not have time to run after their God given dreams; they are too busy trying to make ends meet. If your whole life is just about a chase after money and wealth, you are a poor man. The gospel is what the poor need to show them how to escape from their closets and begin living their real lives.

The poor worry about what they will eat tomorrow; the rich do not worry about that. The poor worry about what to wear tomorrow; the rich only worry about which pair of suit to pick.

Jesus one day addressed this question and he said:

"But seek ye first the kingdom of God, and his righteousness; and all these things shall be added unto you." Mat 6:33

To *"seek first the kingdom of God"* is to pursue God's method and formula for success. It is settled, every person wants to succeed in anything they plan to do; no one plans to fail; the question however is: what method and formula are you using to attain your success? There are so many ways through which you can achieve your goals. Many people have gone to the extent of robbing banks to get money, killing their children to become rich and famous, selling their souls to obtain wealth; and many other weird things. But a man who belongs to the kingdom of God only has one formula: "*to seek first the kingdom of God*". This means to seek the knowledge of the keys that unlock everything you need in life; it means to pursue the kingdom of God. The average Christian thinks to seek the kingdom of God is to always attend church and pray three times a day; this can never be further from the truth.

In other words, concern yourself with the principles of the kingdom of God; pursue righteousness, not unrighteousness, and all these things will not be a worry to you.

To be righteous simply means to be in good terms with God (To not commit sin) it is as simple as that; you do not need a college degree to understand this.

Robert Kiyosaki, in his book with Donald Trump "*Why we want you to be rich*", says these words and I quote:

"*In business, I have a strong faith that if I work with the highest good and fulfil a mission, a higher calling, I will enlist the powers of a Supreme Being. I believe that if I cheat, lie or am not forthright, I diminish the power of what Native Americans refer to as the Great Spirit. I also believe the more I strive to work at the highest legal, ethical and moral standards, the more the power of the Great Spirit enters my business*".

The people need to be taught these kingdom principles, and then they will stop worrying and will replace it with principles that work. Worry has never produced a miracle, but it can surely produce death.

Are you financially asleep or awake?

Chapter 9

To do is greater than to have

What good is knowledge if you cannot use it?

What good is knowledge if you cannot apply it? What good is faith if you cannot use it?
How many books have you read and what percentage of that have you actually put to use?

The greatest obstacle to success is not lack of knowledge, it is when knowledge that has been learned cannot be put to use. When no action is followed up on your knowledge, when you cannot practice what you preach, you are not different from one that is still in darkness, unless your knowledge is applied.

Show me your faith without works, and I will show you my faith by what I do.

Knowledge in itself will not guarantee you a successful life. Education is only a means to your success, not an end.
In the same way that you expect a student after he completes his studies, to look for a job and start working to apply his skills, is the very same way knowledge must be treated.

I have come to discover that so very often, it is not because people do not know what to do or how to do it that they are in their unfortunate circumstances, but in many cases, it is just a mere fact of non-responsiveness to what they know to do.

It is a very tragic thing when you observe our folk in the

teaching profession. They have a greater responsibility of demonstrating the knowledge they teach. A teacher is a carrier of knowledge and information and yet very few of these teachers actually apply the knowledge in the real world. Of what benefit is it to teach the world about how to make money when you cannot use the same knowledge for yourself?

How can the world trust a chain smoker who is teaching *"The 7 steps to quit smoking"*?
How can anyone trust a divorcee who's teaching *"10 Steps to a successful marriage"*?

Knowledge is of no effect if you lack the drive to apply it in your life. People who never try what they learn can never be true leaders – they disguise themselves as leaders but inside, they are truly followers.
How can you know whether what you claim to know is the truth unless you put it to test? A theory that cannot be proved only becomes a theorem. If you do not put your education to test, your education reduces to a theorem.

I once had a lecturer who taught us computer software programming. This man was so good at teaching it hurt to see him beg for a lift every day because he couldn't afford to buy a car for so long!!
I discovered that though he was excellent at lecturing, he had never applied this knowledge for himself to develop a software system that he could easily sell and buy himself a car. His income was only from a small salary that the school that employed him would give at the end of each month.

Nevertheless, I picked up the skills from him and immediate-

-ly started trying them out on the market; I put them to test without reservations, and within no time, in one project that lasted for two months, I made over $10,000 – an amount which my lecturer only made annually at that time.

There is a common saying that *Knowledge is power* – the truth is; knowledge is not power unless that knowledge is applied – Applied knowledge is power.

The other day I asked my friend what his resolutions for the New Year were. He told me, he's been making resolutions every year and they keep piling up, the only resolution he can make for now is to make sure the past resolutions are all implemented.

There is only one step remaining to your success – DO IT.

It's one thing to have knowledge, but it's completely another thing to do the knowledge. Our Age is called *The Knowledge Age* or The *information Age*. There has never been an era in the history of the world when there was so much knowledge everywhere than the era we are living in today.

Today, knowledge is what determines how competitive you are; and the world measures your knowledge by your education status.

If you hold a certificate, you are not as competitive as the one who holds a diploma. If you hold a diploma, you are not as competitive as the one who holds a bachelor's degree. If you hold a bachelor's degree, you are not as competitive as the one who holds a master's degree – and it progresses like that.

The prophet Daniel many years ago prophesied that, in the last days, knowledge shall increase. But the bible also says that knowledge puffs up. In other words, knowledge will make you feel big. However, no matter how knowledgeable you are or how big you feel, if that knowledge cannot be transformed into action, you are not different from a big balloon full of air.

Let your life pick the fruits of your knowledge by the action you do.

Are you financially asleep or awake?

Chapter 9

If you neglect knowledge and despise education, you are abandoning your future

You can never have what you cannot see

$\mathscr{Y}$our ability to see, determines the confidence in your step to move forward. The less you see where you are going, the lesser the progress you will make to advance.

The bible says:

"In the beginning, God created the heavens and the earth."
Genesis 1:1

"And God said, let there be light: and there was light. " Genesis 1:3

God called the light day and the darkness he called night. This was created on the first day.
On the second and third day, God created dry land and the plants and he divided the dry land from the sky – and he saw that it was good.
On the fourth day, he started putting lights in the sky (this is what we call stars). He also made two great lights, the sun and the moon for planet earth. One to rule the day, while the other to rule the night.
"And God made two great lights; the greater light to rule the day, and the lesser light to rule the night."
Genesis 1:16

What is interesting to note is that God created light on the first day before he created the sun, the moon and the stars on the fourth day. It appears like he created light twice; except the light he created on the *first day, is a different kind of light.* The bible says:

"The entrance of thy words giveth light; it giveth understanding unto the simple. " Psalms 119:130

It also calls those who have not been enlightened by the gospel as the children of darkness while those enlightened are called the children of light. It is clear that the light that God created on the first day is not the physical light we get from the sun and moon, because the sun and the moon were not in existence at this time; the kind of light God created on the first day is not the one that causes us to see with our physical eyes. The kind of light that was created on the first day is the one we call knowledge; the one that causes us to see with our mind.

When you are in the dark and someone switches on the light, you say "I can see!!"
When you don't know something and someone explains it to you, you say "I see".

Before the light of God's knowledge was spoken, confusion reigned on the surface of the earth; the sky was not in its place and the earth did not have a shape (formless); ignorance was king. God spoke knowledge into existence and separated it from ignorance and he saw that it was good. Good enough to begin his creation process. He called ignorance darkness and he called knowledge light.

If you cannot see with your mind, you will not see with your eyes

The number one and most important key in the development of a nation is knowledge and education. If you want to know the future of a nation's development, take a look at its education policy; how much does the nation spend on educating its citizens? What is on the priority list of the government's budget?

A nation that does not widen its perception by educating its citizens is a nation that is short sighted. Education widens your perspective and knowledge increases your vision.

The Jewish nation has been reputed through generations as a wise and highly intellectual people. The Jews possess the greatest number of all Nobel prizes won in the world; Jews currently make up 0.25% of the world's population but have got 23% of all Nobel prizes won in the world since 1901.

Some of the greatest inventions were done by Jewish people. The first atomic bomb was invented and developed by a group of Jewish scientists; and Albert Einstein, a Jew, discovered the famous formula $E=MC^2$. The greatest scientists of our time, such as Albert Einstein, Neil Bohr, and the famous Leonardo Da Vinci all have Jewish origins in them. Even when you are talking about IQ and general intelligence, Einstein is used as a measure and symbol of intelligence.

If you investigate the foundation of Jewish people, you notice some very peculiar customs that were a requirement for every young Jew. Every young Jew was expected to study and memorize the first five books of the bible. This was foundational and was a mark that would enable this nation never to forget the laws of God. This tradition is the first act that is responsible in opening up the mind of the young Jew.

You can never divorce IQ from a people that are so buried into knowledge like the Jewish folk.

Some people may want to ague and say that the Jews are an intellectual people because they are God's elect – in bible days, in the old testament, true, God chose this one nation to demonstrate his power and presence in this earth; they were to be a pointer for all nations to the one true God, Jehovah. However, in the New Testament, God extended his favor to the whole world; we now have what is referred to as the church which is now, just like the Jews, a chosen nation.

"But ye are a chosen generation..." 1 Peter 2:9
This should mean that if all that was needed for a people to have such high IQ was to be chosen by God, then the church should have similar IQ like that of the Jews.

From the existence of Nobel prizes in 1901 to date, the Jews have dominated in all categories. There must be something else that causes this effect on people. Their culture puts knowledge above; it elevates education; and this alone is what makes a nation to shine and reign above the rest.

Are you financially asleep or awake?

Chapter 10

If only I had some capital...

If you have capital, you are already rich

$\mathcal{I}$ have talked to many people who always give this excuse: *"If only I had some capital..."*

Perhaps you are one of these people who cannot step out and stretch themselves because they feel, they don't have enough capital to support their dreams.

I once had a very interesting uncle, who has since passed on. Once in a while I would visit him at his farm house where we would chat about almost anything. My uncle was a very ambitious man, always talking about his big dreams and how he would achieve this and achieve that. One particular dream he had was to cultivate over a thousand hectares of land for his crop. He wasn't a commercial farmer but he had the dream to one day be able to feed the nation from his farm.

So each time I visited him he would be talking about how 'this year' he will plough five hundred hectares of land and plant this crop and that crop; he would fantasize about how many bags of maize he will produce and how much each bag will cost, and he would go on and on and on.

Visit him again at the end of the farming season to see what he did, NOTHING!! He did not have enough capital for his project; and so his dream would always remain a dream. I have met people who have shared with me very brilliant ideas, but the problem is that, that's all they are, brilliant ideas. Ideas will always remain ideas, until they hatch from their present state

The commonest excuse from many idea carriers I have met is that they lack capital to grow their ideas.

Have you ever heard of the phrase *"A journey of a thousand miles begins with one step"*?

If your idea is to build a modern day shopping mall, I doubt how long it would take you if you cannot even build a grocery shop. It's a brilliant thing to have big dreams, but big dreams should be made of little dreams that can be used as building blocks to your ultimate dream.

Your dreams need to be realistic and attainable within your context. While it might not be a big deal for Bill Gates to build a modern day shopping complex, it might be a big dream for you to build a grocery shop. So, let your dreams be realistic, attainable and progressive. In other words, fragment your wild dream into little progressive dreams and begin from there. If your dream is too big even in your eyes, you will never start, and you will always think it will happen some day in the future – the problem is that, future will always be in the future. If your dream is unrealistic even in your eyes, you will never believe in it.

If your dream was someone else's and you were approached to fund it, would you do it if you had the means?

I heard of a story of five software engineering companies that used to build software for various machines and devices. One day, they were all in one seminar room attending a workshop on how to build auto-pilot software for aircrafts. The instructor started by asking them one question:
"If your company was the one that built the software for this aircraft, how many of you would take a flight on the plane?" He asked.

There was total silence for about a minute, and then sluggishly, an old and frail looking man lifted up his hand and exclaimed *"I would!!"*

"Finally, a confident programmer" sighed the instructor.
"What makes you so confident about your programming code?" the instructor further inquired.

"For starters..." the old man mumbled,
"With the programming code I have seen from my company, the aircraft will most definitely never have a chance of rolling on the runway and later on take off. So I know I will be safe on that plane."

What chance do you have of getting funding for your dream, if you do not believe in it yourself? This is where it all begins – believe in your dream, and then others will find it easy to believe in it also. If you really believe in your dream, you need to clearly put it down on paper, explain it as if you were doing it to a first grader. Let your business plan prove that you have a worth while product in the making.

Your brain is your capital.

Your worth on earth is determined by how much of your mind you put to use. The brain is an amazing organ of your body. It's the major component of your mind; the factory of all thoughts, plans, behaviors and indeed the entire personality. Without it, you are worth nothing. Without it, you are not counted as 'normal'; you are not part of the population census of your country. Without it, you will not even be allowed to vote. Without it, your significance on earth is zero.

Your mind is your greatest asset. If someone asks you whether you have lost your mind, they are not trying to be nice to you. They are trying to inform you that whatever you are doing, you did not consult the most important part of your personality – the mind.

All known inventions came through the medium of the mind. All discoveries were made by the mind. All scientific advances are products of the mind.

If the mind therefore, is such an important part of our person, then the mind can be used to generate solutions to our problems.

One of the major obstacles to solutions is the lack of use of the mind. The mind is a tool that can be locked and opened depending on what you feed it.

If you keep feeding your mind with the words *"I can't"* it locks and ceases to operate. But if you keep passing it questions of how you can accomplish the objective, your mind orients itself, and takes a journey in search for the solution.

I have personally experienced solutions coming to me in my sleep, because my mind didn't sleep but went looking for the answers.

I remember one particular instance while at school in my fourth year in the school of engineering – we had an assignment and the topic was on Artificial Intelligence. I had gone through all the literature I had and couldn't figure out what the solution was; my mind could not rest, every moment I turned, I was connecting different pieces together in my mind to come up with a solution, but I never seemed to reach the conclusion. I was so tired; I had to retire to bed.

I hardly hit the bed, when I completely fell into a deep sleep. However, although I was deep in sleep, my mind was wide awake, because I started having a dream. In my dream, the solution to my problem started unfolding – I saw the answer clearly in my sleep. Within a few moments, I was awake and wrote down every detail of what I dreamt.

I later presented this to my lecturer; Lo and behold, I was right – and I had never seen it in any book.

My mind went searching, the best it knows how, and came back with the answer. I am not talking about soul traveling – what I am trying to say here is, if you put your mind to work, it does the job, but if you put it to sleep, it sure takes a good nap.

The problem is not because you do not have capital, but that you have not engaged your mind on how you can obtain that capital.

If you accept your condition of lack which impedes your progress, no one will help you out of that prison. If you do not believe in your dream, you will abandon it and blame lack of capital for not pursuing it.

In the business world, only those with strong backbones survive; those with persuasive resolve to achieve what they intend to achieve. The entire business world is fighting for the common goal – to build financial wealth. Therefore, every opportunity that comes on the plate of any business house, must convincingly promise increased revenue for their business.

The major holder of what you call capital is your bank. The primary goal of any bank or any financial institution for that matter is to maximize their profits through re-investing your money. When your bank collects your money together, the monies are put into some money market instruments which yield interest revenues for the bank.

The other biggest strategy your bank uses, in building its business acumen, is through lending out monies at some lending rate favorable to the bank. When your bank lends out money, the money is paid back not at the same interest rate as when the bank borrows from you, by keeping your money in some fixed deposit account. Therefore lending out money is one of the banks major sources of income. In other words, if the bank does not lend out, the bank is not making money.
The most unbelievable thing to everyone who thinks capital is a big problem is that, your bank is actually waiting to lend you the money. When your bank lends you the money, you are giving business to your bank – they are not doing you a favor, although it appears so.

There is however, what is called *fiduciary*. If your bank does not trust you, you will not see the money – it is common sense, they don't want to lose business. This is true in any human relationship; if two parties can no longer trust each other, the harmony that existed between them is broken.
If your credit rating is questionable, in other words, if you are

a bad debtor who borrows and defaults in repayments, your bank may not likely entertain the idea of lending you the capital.

You will therefore, discover that what is really of importance is a well thought out business plan, your good reputation and the passion to achieve your goals. This will get you your capital.

In dealing with small business owners and their major obstacles to realizing their dreams; I have come to discover that a good percentage of them are impeded by fear – fear that their business ideas may never work; however, most of what we fear turns out to be shadows full of nothing.

It's better to try and fail than to never try at all and succeed
You will never know how successful you would have been if you never try. An old saying goes like this:
He that has never failed has never tried anything new.

So don't allow fear of failure and rejection stop you from taking that first step in releasing your business dreams.

Are you financially asleep or awake?

Chapter 11

You should NEVER give your seed

Your seed is what will produce your next harvest, don't give it away

---

*E*verything under the sun has a purpose, and lack of understanding concerning the purpose of a thing will often result in the abuse or the misuse of it.

A lot of teachings with misinterpretations have gone out to the world on the subject of giving, sowing, planting and reaping.

Give and it shall be given unto you... good measure, pressed down....
God loves a cheerful giver...
For God so loved the world that he gave...
It is more blessed to give than to receive...
The hand that gives shall not hunger but he that withholds shall tend to poverty...

It is a paradox; it's like saying, for you to go left, you must head right; for you to go up, you must head downwards; for you to be happy, you must learn sorrow; for you to sit on the throne, you must first be a slave, for you to have, you must give.

Everything in the kingdom of God works in opposites, and until you can pick this up, you'll be struggling living the kingdom life. People want to do and follow what makes logical sense, but the logic of the kingdom of God is differe-

-nt from the logic of the world. In the world system, giving only happens when you have plenty, and if you have little, spend it on yourself and your family otherwise you'll die of hunger if you give it away.

It is, however, evidently clear that those who often have little and do not practice the art of giving, always tend to have insufficient each time.

In the kingdom of God's system, your generosity opens up doors for you to receive more. Apparently, this system works as a principal law. In other words, you do not have to belong to any religious sect for it to work; whether you are Christian, Moslem, Hindu, Buddhist or even atheist, the principle of giving and receiving works for all; it's more like the law of gravity, whoever jumps, comes down; what you believe at this point does not matter.

Some sects such as the Moslems in our community practice this principle very well. It is practically hard to find a single Muslim stricken with poverty and hunger in a community where other Muslims have plenty to spare. While on the other hand, it is common place for Christians to have some among them literally sleeping on empty stomachs when there are others who are throwing away left over foods.

In trying to bring out the message of giving, many teachers have ended up misleading unsuspecting and innocent people and have painfully dragged multitudes into this wave of ignorance and left those worse than they started.

The message of giving has been so distorted that when you hear it, most times it suggests firstly that; if you do not give money, you have not given; secondly, it suggests that the object of your giving must be the church and the man of

God (or preacher). And most tragic of all, most teachers teach that for God to heal you or answer any form of prayer from you, you must give something to him, as if God were some consultant who only attends to those who pay their consultation fees.

In the early church, the object of giving was to the poor people in the society. The church was encouraged to give to the poor, and not the poor giving to the church. I am not in any way insinuating that you do not have to give to the *church or the preacher;* I am simply inferring the fact that the message has been taught with emphasis on giving to the church rather than giving to the poor.

> *Any church organization that does not give to the poor is simply a profit making organization and should not be upheld at all.*

The only reason you should give to church, is so that the church will in turn use that money to reach the poor. If the church does not have a program to take the message of the gospel of the kingdom to the poor, your giving to this church is equivalent to a donation.

Well, let's get to the subject of the matter; firstly, we need to define what a seed is, and what the purpose of a seed is. Secondly, we will try to distinguish the difference between *giving* and *sowing* because they are not the same.

The word *seed* also means *source* or *origin*. A seed is an element or organism containing all the genetic characteristics of the expected matured life but lives as a single dormant entity. The origin of every living organism comes from a seed. In other words, a seed contains all the traits of its germinated result.

A mango seed contains all the characteristics of a mango tree and cannot yield anything else other than a mango tree.

To understand the purpose of a seed, we will first look at what it is not intended for.

1. *Seed is not for eating (consumption)*

Seed, as the name suggests, is a carrier of the next generation of a species and is therefore, not intended for consumption. A man who consumes his seed will never see a harvest. Consuming your seed terminates the perpetuation of the generation within that seed.

2. *Seed is not for giving*

If you give me your seed and I plant it in my field, whose harvest should it be? Well, common sense tells all of us that it will be my harvest, not yours; after all, you gave me that seed and I became legal owner of all that seed was capable of producing.
This is where, the teaching of giving has been distorted; people give away their seed but remain expecting a harvest. How can you give away, and yet expect a harvest? If you are a giver, you are not expected to live in lack, but abundance comes from sowing. Every spiritual truth must be explained with a natural principle.
If you got all your maize meant for seed and gave it to your brother, and he decided to go plant it in his field, who should be expecting a harvest?
No! no! no!, I am not saying you should not give, hear me well; I am saying, you should not give your seed!! *Giving* is not *sowing*. Giving is simply giving.

What then should a wise man do with his seed?

Jesus once gave a parable of the sower who went out to sow his seed. There's only ONE thing you should do with seed, and that is the sole purpose of every seed on earth. You must sow your seed. To sow also means to plant. Planting is not giving away. To plant also means to invest or to bury for future growth. For any harvest to come to pass, the seed MUST be buried first.

God knew and established this principle. He gave his son away as a seed to the world, but he (GOD) could not expect any harvest until the seed (Jesus) was buried; this was God's investment in order for him to reap the harvest which we now call the church.

"Verily, verily I say unto you, except a corn of wheat fall into the ground and die, it abideth alone: but if it dies, it bringeth forth much fruit." John 12:24

Jesus here was referring to his death and the birth of the church after his burial and resurrection.

A man who has seen his future will sow his seed today

The biggest question therefore is: where do you plant your seed?

Well, firstly we have already established the fact that *giving* is not *planting*. Therefore, if you give your seed to the poor (the poor man eats your seed), you are not planting, you are just giving – in short, you are misusing your seed because, you have not utilized it for its intended purpose.

What about giving seed to church? I am sure up to this point I have clearly distinguished the difference between giving and sowing. When you give your seed to church, you are not planting, you are just giving. There's a giving and there's a planting and the two cannot be the same.

Most people do not know when to give and when to plant. When you give, and you must give, you should not expect a harvest of returns; because giving is an expression of your love, respect and hornor. When you give to express your love, it's immoral to start waiting for a bumper harvest from your giving. Because of lack of understanding, many people have ended up trading with God.

Giving is not seasonal, in other words, there is no special season in which you should give; and when men give back to you, it does not return to you in a specific season. In short, you cannot give in January and expect to receive back in March. The law of giving is this: if you give, people will give you also, if you don't, people will not give you also; that's why the bible says, give and shall be given unto you – it therefore becomes common sense that we can say; *don't give and it shall not be given unto you also* - this is a law of giving - not of planting.

Investing or sowing or planting however, is not an expression of your love; this is a business transaction.
When you plant your seed, you must expect a harvest at a definite time and season, it's not a requirement for you to exercise your faith in order to receive your harvest. Just plant your seed and in due time, it will yield your harvest.
A farmer knows when to plant his maize seed, and when to expect to reap the harvest.

Many people have given their seed and because they thought

they had planted, they started waiting in faith to receive a harvest which in most cases was not forth coming. These genuine people have ended up blaming themselves into thinking that they either did not have enough faith or enough patience, when in actual fact, what they didn't have was enough knowledge on the subject. Others have blamed God altogether while others have lost confidence in the men of God they trusted.

I met a grown man who has vowed not to ever give his money to church because, he felt tricked when he was compelled to give his money, meant as capital for his small business, to church. He felt compelled after the preacher talked about sowing into the church and believed that God was going to reward him back a hundred fold (He's still waiting for the returns and getting very angry for the delay).

I am yet to find a scripture that supports the idea of giving a certain amount to a church or to a man of God in order for God to meet your needs. My stand on this is: these are doctrines of men and mostly tailored to deprive poor people of becoming the great men they were meant to be. God can never be contained in a box; just because a widow in the bible gave her last bread to Elijah the prophet and God gave her constant supplies, does not mean that every widow must find a man of God and give him her last penny in order to get a constant supply of pennies.

Simply giving your money to someone and sitting down to expect 1000% interest on returns the following month is utter laziness and should not be encouraged. The church offering bag is not some magic box where you throw in a dollar today and pull out a $1000 the next day. God's government is not out there running government bonds at astronomical interest returns. If it were, all one needs to start with is 1 dollar, and they'll be a billionaire the following year.

Getting your seed money and giving it away is misusing the purpose for seed.

I am not advocating that people should stop supporting the church financially to propagate the gospel, but the methods and ways used for this purpose are very wrong.
Is it possible that God would expect me to give $1000 in order to receive an answer to my prayer?
Well, you cannot put God in a box, he's capable of anything; however, the rate at which god is demanding these monies is alarming.

People of God, be wise – if God has given you his son and eternal life without paying for it, do you honestly think he would withhold your healing for a thousand dollars? What is your healing compared to eternal life? You must be stingy and stubborn for God to do this – and if he does it to you, then perhaps you must check your giving habits.

The church exists for a purpose, and its purpose is to bring in a harvest of souls. When Jesus explained the parable of the sower to his disciples, he said to them "… *and the seed is the word of God*".

Today, whenever you hear the word seed, it's referring to money. If you want a harvest of money, stop trading in the house of God; take that money and invest it in other money instruments. If you want a harvest of souls, invest your money in church so the church can be empowered to bring in this harvest. Do not trade in church and turn the house of God into a merchandising place. If God wants you to plant your seed in a ministry or church, listen to him and obey his voice because great is the reward if you do this; but do not allow any man to coerce you into sowing into his church or ministry; let God alone coerce you into doing this.

The key message is: your seed is for investment, for planting in your field so you can reap a harvest and from there you can give part. You don't give to yourself, you give to others; but you invest for yourself not for others.

Are you financially asleep or awake?

Chapter 12

Your gift is your wealth

Breaking the paradigm of employment

"A man's gift makes room for him, and brings him before great men." Pro 18:16

I grew up in a society that believed that a man's future lied in his performance at school. My father would always shower you with all kinds of gifts and presents if you were the best in class. No matter how many goals you scored at your local football team, you dare not tell your father that you were out playing football – don't mention it that you were a member of a singing group that sometimes performs at a youth club.

All these are what make you dull!! He would say.
You will never amount to anything if that's the path you want to follow.

These were the words that kept echoing the walls in the rooms we lived. We were literally forced to cement our heads to our books and nothing else.
In my parents' mind, this was the best they could do to shape their children's future. They had observed from other families whose children were nothing to boast home about

because they had neglected school and instead chose 'games'. My parents were only doing the best they knew how.

A few decades ago, this was great advice – but times have now changed, and so should our strategies. Education alone can no longer guarantee a successful life. But education with respect to your gifts and talents is what will set you apart.

Every parent has a God given mandate to train up their children in the way they should go. Every child has his or her peculiar way he/she should go. In other words, the specifics of a child's purpose in life are hidden within the child and they begin to show up slowly as the child grows. The parent's responsibility is to detect this, and guide the child to begin the journey through this path.

"As arrows are in the hand of a mighty man; so are children of the youth." Psalm 127.4

An arrow cannot serve its purpose until it's properly guided to hit its intended target by the man holding the arrow. In other words, your children need to be properly guided in the way they should grow – in their purpose so they can become the great men they were meant to be.

The greatest tragedy however, is that most parents need this guidance just as much as their children do.

Many parents do not realize this awesome responsibility on them, and therefore we end up with a massive population of people who are unclear about their purpose in life. My parents only knew one way for all children – school.

School is very important; I uphold my parents for promoting education as the primary key to a child's success, but education without knowledge is useless. This might sound paradoxical, how can you be educated and yet be without knowledge?

Our school system collects all different kids together in what they call a classroom and tests them collectively.

Those that make it through the test are called brilliant and supposedly have a successful future ahead of them; the ones that don't manage the test are classified as failures. This is more like collecting different gasses together and subjecting them to an oxygen test.

Of course only the oxygen gas will pass the test. In our current society, the role of the parent in guiding the child to its destiny is crucial. Many parents surrender their children to the school system and expect the school system to bring out a king out of their son or a queen out of their daughter. Education alone does not bring you before great men. It's your gift which you have developed with the help of education that opens the way for you.

Your gift is what should guide your education, not the other way round. In other words, if you are a musician, attend a musical school to improve your musical skills; if you are a doctor, go and study medicine; if you are a writer, take a course in writing. Instead of letting our identity define our education, we have let education define our identity; you are called a lawyer because you went to law school; you are called an economist because you studied economics; you are called an engineer because you studied engineering... the whole system is upside down; you are supposed to go to law school because you are a lawyer; you are supposed to go and study medicine because you are a physician; you are supposed to go and study engineering because you are an engineer.

Whatever your gift is, let education help you sharpen it. This is what I call *guided education*. Education that is unguided is what produces average and unmotivated employees. Many kids attend tertiary education before they ever find out who they are, and so they end up doing what is not relevant to their purpose in life.

Your greatness will not be achieved through education alone – it's that education that sharpens your gift which produces the great man in you.

Examples of some great men of our time today and the lessons we pick from their lives:

Nelson Madiba Mandela

Mandela saw, a long time ago, what everyone else never saw. He had a vision of a free South Africa where black people would dwell in harmony with white people. He saw the death of apartheid and racism long before it came to pass. Nothing and no one could swerve him away from his focus; he was willing to go to prison and even to die as the price he could pay for what he saw in his spirit. He was born for this very purpose and nothing could stop him, not even death. This kind of passion and resolve is derived from his love for his leadership gift in him. Mandela is a true leader that pursued his gift with great intensity and his gift truly brought him before great men.

True leaders do not possess revengeful spirits. Many African leaders swept their independent nations off of white people immediately they became independent. They repossessed and nationalized white people's businesses in the spirit of hatred and revenge. They took up leadership positions without true leadership qualities, and as a result, many African countries were plunged in a state of wantonness and poverty.

What can we pick from this great man called Mandela?
The man knew his gift, his vision was clear to him. If a man is willing to go to prison for twenty seven (27) years and even to die for his cause, this man is not joking; you better hear him out.

Bill Gates and Steve Jobs

They may have been rivals, but I put them together here. One is boss of Microsoft and the other of Apple.
We live in the information age – it's no longer how strong you are that matters, but what you know, that determines the difference between a successful life and a troubled one.
Bill Gates and Steve Jobs, in their respective carriers, have shaped the way this age looks at life and business in general and you can never get that away from them.

Their great inventions determine the success and failure of many organizations today. They are both a very good example of the fact that education alone no longer guarantees a successful life.
Bill Gates and Steve Jobs dropped out of formal school to pursue their dreams, and were committed to these dreams until they started paying them off – Bill Gates is one of the richest men on earth as far as money is concerned.
I don't recommend that you should drop out of school and run after your dreams like Bill and Steve did, I simply use the illustration as an example to show that it's not education

alone that will bring you before great men; it's your gift – your educated gift that creates a throne for you. If Tiger Woods' parents prevented him from playing golf from his childhood and instead forced him to only pay attention to his education – only to study accountancy for instance, today we would not have known the Tiger Woods we have come to know now. He would have been an accountant in a firm somewhere living below his normal potential – living someone else's dream, fighting for a pay raise.

What is your gift?
Let's do a little exercise. In the world today, many people derive their identities from the careers which school gave them at the end of all those merciless exams.

Pele, Ronaldinho and Tiger Woods

Scandals aside, some names are synonymous to certain activities. Whenever you mention the name Pele or Ronaldinho, the first thing that comes to mind is soccer. Whenever you think about golf, you also think about Tiger Woods and vice versa; you cannot divorce the two. These men know what their gifts are and it shows. It is this gift in them which makes them take place among great men. If Tiger Woods should go to school, it must be to sharpen his skills in golf or to help him manage this gift effectively.

We have engineers, doctors, lawyers, scientists, accountants, nurses, and teachers and so on; and all these identities are because you passed those exams; had you failed them, that identity wouldn't be on you today. I would like you to take a piece of paper and on it, write down who you think you are irrespective of how school defined you. Describe yourself fully in a paragraph; take a moment to think only about you. Describe your gifts and talents, your personality and character.

Now, read through what you wrote about you, and put it down again in point form.

Is what you are currently pursuing related to who you are?

What do you need to change to begin living in the direction of yourself?

When you go to bed tonight, go thinking about those words you wrote about yourself; memorize each word and say it back to yourself. Do this until your sub conscious mind gets it.

It is a very tragic thing to think you are an engineer when in fact you are a writer. You need to re-brain wash yourself by feeding your mind with your correct identity.

Some people call themselves nurses when actually inside they are doctors; they have always dreamt of becoming doctors, but those exams deprived them of this identity and so they accepted another identity of nurse.

When Jesus was born, his identity was *"savior of the world"* what is yours?

Are you financially asleep or awake?

Chapter 13

Understanding the value of time

Time is very far from what your watch actually reads

"To everything, there is a season and a time *to every purpose under heaven."* Eccl 3:12

$\mathcal{N}$othing and no one lives forever here on earth. Every human has a time limit enclosed between the beginning of his life and the end of his life; and within this limit, there exists seasons to man that are capable of producing impeccable results of everything he does if utilized properly. Nature will not always give you the rainy season, winter does not last forever – but a fool will go out to plant when it's time to harvest, he will begin to sow when the rain is saying "goodbye".

No one will go out into his field to harvest his crop if he knows very well that he did not plant anything; also you should not expect your crops to grow to maturity, if you planted your seeds on the last day of the rains of the season. Opportunities happen to all people, but only the wise understand that some opportunities come only once in a life time and they are not an every day occurrence; so if you do not act within the presentation of this chance, you may never get it again.

Time is the greatest asset given to man but an asset that has been widely mismanaged.
If I asked you what time it is now; you'll probably quickly

answer me "11:30hrs" or "14.20hrs" or whatever your wrist watch says – but chances are that you have no clue exactly what time it really is for you. Time, though generally measured by your geographical location, was not meant to be a general dimension common to people within a location.

It is tragic that so many people have no idea whether it's time to sleep, time to plant, time to study, time to play, time to give or time to learn. For many, all these events occur haphazardly, giving nature the right to control their time – what a tragedy indeed.

So most people sleep because the sun has gone down, they study because they have an exam, they play because their friends have come, they give because they have too much and all activities in their schedules are orchestrated by external forces. To such a person, when a life time opportunity presents if self, it usually finds them not ready and slips away leaving them in a continuous state of mediocrity.

A person, who does not know how to use his time, is a person who has no respect for his future.

The most dreadful thing that the youth of our time face now is the uncertainty of what the future holds and the fear of what tomorrow brings. Our society has even coined phrases such as "*There's no light at the end of the tunnel*" meaning your days coming ahead are as dark and uncertain as pitch darkness in hell.

We live in a world where pain and hurt has become our closest friends; poverty is accepted as a way of life; sickness and disease is regarded as normal and when it takes our lives or those of our loved ones, we accept it as the will of God. HIV & AIDS has been given the right to rob us of our future

105

We live in a world where we have allowed unemployment to become the source of our depression.

Terrorism has created boundaries which have enslaved us and limited our expansions and expectations; and the moment with think about tomorrow, the thought comes with all kinds of fears. Well, then, how can you tell what time it really is for you and not let the cares and worries overtake you? 12.00hrs to me may not be exactly 12.0hrs to you – in other words, my winter may occur at the same time your summer is occurring. The challenge is; how do you tell in what season you are?

This alone is a million dollar question, and the lack of this understanding is one of the major causes of poverty to many.

No one can tell you what time it really is better than you can tell yourself. You need to realize that your whole life is unique and it was a process that was started to eventually produce a king. Constantly failing to recognize what time it is in your life, will eventually result in the abortion of this process.

People can only go as far as confirming what time it is for you; the responsibility of reading the time lies totally with you.

Why is reading the time so important? Your time is connected to your purpose; if you miss your time, you'll miss your purpose and life will become just one long stretch of frustrations.

Remember this:

"To everything, there is a season and a **time to every purpose** under heaven."

People that end their lives are people who never knew their

purpose for living; it is dangerous to live near such people.

Whether you have recognized it or not, your entire life cries only for one thing; to become 'MASTER'. In other words, your life yearns to excel in your gifts and talents to such proportions that the world will begin to recognize you as 'The Great', like Alexander the great, Albert Einstein, Sir Isaac Newton, Leonardo Da Vinci, Ayn Rand, Peter Russell, Galileo Galilee, John F Kennedy, Nelson Mandela and the list goes on…

The desire to become great is a very godly desire, so do not thwart it, but nature it because your greatness is meant for the benefit of the human race. There wouldn't be a great history without great people of history.

If your dream is to become the best doctor in your country "Doctor Jerry the great", having six of your best friends and none of them a doctor, is a direct attack to your dream and time.

"Every purpose is established by counsel: and with good advice make war."
Prov.20:18

The world is full of disoriented youngsters and adults who do not know exactly the reason for their existence – and because of this, can not fully explore their greatness; they eventually end up as copy cats, imitating other people and only becoming average humans.

Discovering the reason or purpose for your life is your number one and most important assignment on earth.

Every purpose is established by counsel. In other words, if you do not yet know the reason for your existence, you need counsel to establish it in your life. Many books have been written about how to discover your purpose in life; young people struggle with this question and adults fail to give any clear answers because they are also faced with the same question, but the greatest and simplest solution to this world wide question is just in one word... counsel.

The word counsel means to give direction; it also means to mentor or to steer. You might wonder, 'what has this got to do with being financially awake?' EVERYTHING!! Because your life is meant to be driven by purpose and NOT finance.

Lack of purpose to your life will often result to lack of purpose to your finance.

Most people just follow the direction of events in their lives instead of giving direction to the events. They do not have a clear direction on what to pursue with passion. They are not sure whether they are footballers or singers or just actors; so they swing from one thing to another thing. Millions of people live their lives without giving serious thought to whether the way they are living is the way they ought to be living.

Every person has an inner mentor voice that holds the key to the direction ones life ought to take.

Some people are passionate about doing something and becoming someone but have no idea how. This is why you have this book in your hands!! To give you pointers to a life worth living, a life of greatness.

If you are in the category of those who are not sure who they are, who can not find passion in anything or have not just explored to discover themselves and live passionately, you must be congratulated for reading this book this far, at least it shows that you are passionate about knowledge. Let's call this Category 1.

If knowledge is the last thing on your agenda, you will never know what hit you!!

For those in Category 1, I will show you how to practically start putting meaning to your life, how to find passion in life and die for it. You cannot be truly passionate about anything until you can die for it. Life does not have a meaning until you find what you can die for.

Let me ask you some simple, yet very important questions, and I would like you to take time to seriously think before answering them.

....

Can you truly tell me that you do not admire to be like anybody you have seen, come in contact with or read about so far? Simply put, do you admire to be like somebody you know?

Can you truly tell me that you do not have any gifts or talents in you? Can you tell me that nothing and no one inspires you at all?

I would like you to do something for yourself – for now, it may seen to be for yourself, but later, you will discover that what you did was the biggest first step you ever made in touching the world.

Here is *what I would like you to do:*
Put a bookmark on this page and take a couple of days leave from it; during this period, I would like you to answer the questions above in all honesty and truth to yourself and for the benefit of all those who are connected to your destiny.

1. Think deeply about what truly inspires you – something that you'd love doing even if you are not paid for it (*I didn't hear you say eating….??*)
2. Jokes aside, write down the names of all those people who are already successfully doing this thing or living this life or those who have already gone through this path before.
3. Ask yourself genuinely whether this is what you would love to be.
 Do not focus on the results (*the fame, the wealth etc*).

When you establish these facts, fight like heck to get the biographies of these people. Thoroughly read through their biographies; their achievements, their failures, their hobbies… and carefully choose one who will act as your *mentor.*

Your next step will be to wisely develop a relationship with your mentor. You might think, "*wait a minute here, what if this mentor is thousands of miles from here, or maybe they are even dead, how do I develop this relationship with a celebrity who I might never get to meet?*"

You can develop a relationship with Leonardo Da Vinci, for though the world thinks Da Vinci is dead, his spirit still lives on through his works. Great people never die; that is why your spirit cries for greatness, it was never created to die. In other words, your mentor lives through his work; his books, his songs, his paintings, his theories etc. Develop this relationship with your mentor.

This mentor, through his work, will be the one who will steer up, give direction and counsel you to establish that purpose for your life. The great advice you will obtain from this mentor-ship association will be the weaponry you will use to war your way into greatness. And do not settle for anything less than the very best.

If you cannot do this, I'll tell you only one thing: laziness will never pay you a cent and you probably need to pass on this book because knowledge without action is like a bird that cannot fly, it's like a fish that cannot swim and that bird or fish should never have been born.

The Apostle Paul once said *"imitate me as I imitate Christ"* – This is the essence of mentor-ship.

No one is born great, but everyone is born with the potential to become great; many die without realizing and releasing that potential. Dr Myles Munroe refers to this as *adding to the wealth of the cemetery.*

If you fall in the category of those who seem to be passionate about something and would like to become someone but do not know how, here is what I would like you to do: First let's call this Category 2

Write down ten (10) names of those already living your dream life. Pick out the best three and study their biographies, read all their books. In other words, begin tapping into their minds. The mind is the only thing you have that has all the keys to your future and your greatness, and it is the only difference between you and those ten people you wrote down on a piece of paper. The value of your life is directly proportional to the value of your mind.

To achieve what your mentor has achieved, you need to have the mind-set of your mentor which will allow you to think like your mentor.

What am I asking you to do? I am asking you to MODEL your life like that of your mentor.

You have the ability to reproduce all the achievements of your mentor only if you can model your life like his or hers.

Time will not wait for you to first figure out who you are before it starts ticking on you.

Being successful does not mean having millions in your bank account neither does it mean living a better life than your peers. Success is only measured by how much you have become of all that you can become. In other words, success is a measure of what you are, compared to what you are capable of becoming, what you have done compared against what you are capable of doing. Success is only measured against yourself.

If you are a bird that should fly but cannot fly, it would be unreasonable for you to think you are successful because you can run faster than a chicken. The truth is, you are a failure because, you were meant to fly but cannot fly.

Are you financially asleep or awake?

Chapter 14

Know the rules and play the game

In every game, you win or lose; the secret is to know the rules

*E*very game has a standard set of rules, and in every game, sometimes you'll win and sometimes you'll lose. The game of money also has rules, if you do not abide by the rules, you will lose.

Just like the rules in any other game, the rules in the game of money need to be thoroughly understood before you can effectively participate in the game.

Most people, who do not understand the first thing about investing, want to engage in world class investments and reap their benefits the following month. Unfortunately, the game of money is a very emotional game and those without investment stamina often end up nursing unnecessary wounds in their lives.

In my country, soccer is the most popular game. You can almost feel the wave of anxiety in everyone's eyes when their favorite teams are playing. The dampening atmosphere that blankets cliques if their team is losing. The brightness and joy on faces of those supporting the winners. It's undoubtedly clear that soccer is a very emotional game in my country; it makes best of friends and equally creates enemies. However, even if soccer is so popular, not everyone plays the game. Those who are selected as team members are thoroughly acquainted with the rules governing the game – none among the players is expected to confuse soccer rules with basketball rules, wow!! This would be unpardonable. Anybody who violates the rules would either receive a warning from the referee, or would get a red card and be sent off the pitch.

The game of money is more emotional than that of soccer. Unfortunately, the game of money does not have a referee per say; so everyone is a player; some are using 'soccer rules' others are using 'basketball rules' while others are just guessing and somehow hoping that they emerge miraculously as winners. The bottom line is, everyone is expecting to come out as a winner; and for most, if for the first or second time they do not emerge as 'winners' they quickly, with intense emotions, hung up the gloves and immediately appoint themselves as investment advisors to advise the world on why investing is so risky and why it doesn't work.

THE 5 PRINCIPAL RULES OF THE GAME OF MONEY
A) *Money starts as an idea in your mind*
Money is an illusion, it exists only in your mind and when you realize that it is just an idea in your mind, you will know for sure that you can create it at will. Your perception of money will largely determine your attitude towards it.

Money is not that nicely decorated piece of paper bearing the portrait of a dead president; it is anything that is generally acceptable in exchange for goods and services; money does not necessarily need to have an intrinsic value to serve as a medium of exchange. It is someone's willingness to accept it in payment that gives money its value in the exchange process.

When you truly grasp this concept, you will know beyond any doubt that you ALWAYS have money locked up within yourself; the only difference is that the money in you exists in another form other than that nicely decorated paper you have always called money. In other words, money exists in many forms and can therefore be converted into any other form you wish. That's why you need to pay attention to the ideas in your mind, because they are the original form in which money exists.

Do not despise and ignore your ideas, if everyone treated their ideas this way, the world would never have known civilization.

No idea is too small to be natured.

Money really represents the value of a thing; therefore what your mind perceives as either expensive or cheap, your mind will place a value on, and determine the price of. In short, how you value something will determine the price you will put on it.

The ideas in your mind do not hold any determinable value until they are converted into goods or services. All large corporations and companies around you started as an idea in someone's mind. The job you have is because someone did not ignore that little idea they had in their mind, now you are getting paid for it.

Ideas, therefore, are products of your mind, and if they are, which they are, then what you see with your mind is more important than what you see with your eyes. What your mind sees, will eventually determine what your eyes will see.

Two people looking at the same event might see two completely different scenes. One might see a tragedy while the other sees an opportunity. One might see a problem, the other may see a solution, yet both of them are looking at the same thing. Train your mind to see beyond the box, do not under-rate your thoughts, conglomerates are products of thoughts that were natured and given a chance to grow.

If you keep ignoring your 'small' ideas and not give them a chance to prove their worth, you deserve to die a poor man

Imagination is never monopolized; but it is a source from which ideas spring. Begin to take moments in your time to imagine how you want your life to be. In other words, begin to day-dream; picture yourself on top, reigning as a king. Put yourself in the shoes of those you admire (the truth is everyone you admire to be like is above you).

Let your mind fantasize about your future and let it bring out those ideas of how to get there. That's where your money is. This is what will make you happy; and when you are happy, the people around you are happy.

b) Reduce your indebtedness increase those indebted to you
In the game of money, it is how many people you owe versus how many people owe you that determines whether you will win or lose. The more indebted you are, the poorer you'll

become; and the more indebted people are to you, the richer you will become; it is as simple as that.

This is the foundation of what accountants call The Balance Sheet. The list of people you owe is referred to as Liabilities, and the list of people that owe you is referred to as Assets.
The difference between your assets and your liabilities will show you a picture of whether you are headed for wealth or for hail.

Many people struggle with the idea of what an asset is and what a liability is; and because of this misunderstanding, many don't really know whether they are acquiring assets or acquiring liabilities when they do their shopping. This concept alone if not correctly understood, can lead you into a lot of trouble with debt.
Many endow themselves with all kinds of toys and goodies and mistakenly call them assets but are in fact liabilities that keep sucking on them all day long.

According to a very simplified description, which I like, by Robert Kiyosaki from his book "*Rich Dad Poor Dad*", an asset will always generate income for you, while a liability will always demand income from you; this is as simple as it can get. Next time you decide to acquire an asset, ask yourself this question:
"*Will it be paying me or will I be paying it?*"

We were young, fresh from university and excited about life and its challenges. A colleague I met while at school had become my close
close acquaintance and luckily we both ended up settling in the same town. He is the competitive type, from school times

to industrial freshmen, he is the type that wants to show off and prove that he's better than yo.

One day he told me he has managed to acquire all the assets he needed to complete a home. *"Oh! Assets like what?"* I asked him.

"I got that double door gold fridge, a 52 inch television set, leather sofas and oh!! You should come and checkout my sub-woofer stereo…!!, man, it's the one!!"

Now, obviously my friend had been listening to father Christmas a lot looking at the list of items he calls assets. Don't get me wrong here, there is nothing wrong with all these items; they are wonderful and necessary to have. It's the way he kept referring to them as assets that kept bothering me, and unfortunately, many people acquire these wonderful things and list them on their assets list. Our educated friends even give them a special name called fixed assets. Problem is, they are too fixed, and if not careful, they might fix you also.

With our simple definition of an asset and a liability, let's take for instance a double-door fridge for my friend. It is very clear that this item had no salary for him, but it required a salary from him – he needed to fill it up every month, which is good, but the cash was not coming out of the back of the fridge, his pocket was doing it. That electricity it was consuming for preserving its contents does not come for free, his pocket shrunk even further.

What about the 52 inch TV set? Well, it needed picture, good picture, so someone's going to get paid for supplying that picture, and guess who's paying; his pocket of course.

As if that was not enough, my colleague went on to get a mortgage for a house with his new family. Oh, by the way, I did a little dig up on the word mortgage and found that it's actually a combination of two words; A French word *mortia* which means *'death',* and an English word *engagement.* The derived meaning of the word mortgage therefore is: engagement until death.

So, anyway, now my friend has another debt to hopefully clear in the next fifteen (15) years, or is it until death? And you thought that was all? No, he needed transport now that he had a wife. Remember, he wants to show you he's the best, so his car is not a three wheeler, but he gets another four years of imprisonment to clear its debt.

The stage at which my colleague had reached was one at which he could not afford to quit his job either voluntarily or otherwise. The moment he loses his job, all his so called assets will begin to eat him up.

Instead of increasing the number of those who owe him, my colleague had successfully ballooned the number of those he owed by acquiring his assets.

My colleague is not the only one who has found himself in this predicament. Millions of people are suffering peacefully in this rut, and they think the only solution is to work harder and harder to somehow pay off some of those 'assets'. Some have found themselves as victims of company down-sizing and even end up dying younger due to the pressure which they fail to contain.

Remember, your system was never wired to live in pain and pressure, so if you continuously subject it to this environment, it will give in.

119

The most frequent source of frustrations, bad temper, heart attacks,
divorces and the like, come from income management problems.

You are probably wondering, 'what items should I acquire
then to list on my assets column?' remember the simple rule;
assets will always generate income for you.

There are three different options to choose from:

i) Start a small business and make it grow

A business is an entity setup with the sore purpose of
generating income for the owner or owners.

Whatever a business does, whatever products it makes or
whatever services it offers; the primary reason for its
existence is to create money; this is the life line of every
business, and this alone is what qualifies it to be called an
asset.

To most people, the idea of forming a business scares them
out of their socks; a business is just a legal piece of paper
with your company name on it, allowing you to do some
form of trading. It is not that nicely decorated building
swallowing all those nice people from Monday to Friday.

Also, remember that business is not defined as the way to
make money. Business is your ability to produce value which
other people need. It is not money that you need, remember
money is an illusion, you need things but those things have
value on them. In other words, we can replace the word
money with the word value.

Your ability to produce things of value to others is what is called
BUSINESS.

ii) Buy into some profit making business

To participate in sharing of the profits and revenues of a company, you do not necessarily need to start that company. You can buy into a company.

The major difference between rich people and average people is this:

While everyone is rushing to buy products from a company, the rich minded are rushing to buy the company that makes the product. I call them rich not because they have lots of money, but because they think differently, which is why they also have lots of money.

One of the ways the rich buy into a business is through acquiring shares or stocks in the company. Buying stock in a company qualifies you to share in the profits of the company. Unfortunately, if the company makes losses, you share that too.

Everyone goes to a market of some sort, but only a few go to a stock market, very few even know how to buy and sell from this market.

Remember, your ignorance will always cost you.

If you do not sale anything, you will always be a poor man. Learn about buying and selling at the stock market.

iii) *Invest in property*
There is a whole story on how you can build your real estate assets, slowly and painlessly without negatively affecting your cash flow.

iv) *Inventions and papers*
Here, am referring to royalties, mutual funds, pension funds, patents etc. This is where your creativity pays you from. Don't waste your ideas; remember they are the original form in which money exists.

The only way to reduce your indebtedness and increase those indebted to you is when you start investing in real assets. These assets are capable of generating you income to buy those luxuries you were calling assets. Never borrow to go and buy a liability or a luxury; let your assets buy you the luxuries.

There is no magic to resolving your cash flow problems, the secret is this; spend less than what you earn and invest the difference. You need to be very clear during your buying or shopping, whether what you are doing is spending or investing.

Each time you buy an asset, you are investing, and each time you buy a liability, you are spending.

c) Be a member of the winning team

Lone rangers are for entertainment in movies, real life flourishes with teams.

Napoleon Hill, in his book deals squarely with the subject of 'The power of association'. People who have truly succeeded, have not done so entirely on their own. I can never emphasize this point enough; Napoleon puts it this way:

The first and most important thing in the achievement of your goals is this: A burning desire to achieve the set goals and a mastermind group that helps you to achieve this.

A success team is also known as a mastermind group. This group must possess the following qualities:

1. *Character*

You don't want to link up with a crook. The character of a person is key in any relationship. This must come on top of every quality you are looking for in a partner, mentor or associate. Even in business, you must be trusted to succeed. Good character builds a strong name, but a bad character can collapse an empire in a day. All the members in your mastermind group must be of unquestionable character; trustworthy and dependable. One bad egg doesn't go well for the entire omelette. Even among crooks, there's some level of trust-worthiness; in genuine business, bad character will hand you over to the law but among the gangs, bad character will make you lose your knee caps.

2. *Influence*
You want to partner with people who have a good influence on the society, people who are influential in their area. Choose the best and belong to them. It is impossible to be a leader with no influence. Someone said; a leader with no followers is simply a man taking a walk. John Maxwell defines leadership as influence.

3. *IQ*
The IQ of a mastermind group will determine the extent to which the group will go.
This will also determine how influential the group can be. Find these people, partner with these people. Alas, if you are the smartest in the group. You need to surround yourself with people who are smarter than yourself; that is called wisdom.

4. *Beliefs*
The most difficult thing to do is when you have opposing

views in your beliefs and yet you are partners of the same mastermind group. This is not encouraged at all. You need to be supportive of each other and not in opposition with your mates. Find grounds on which you both agree and never tread on controversies as far as beliefs are concerned; especially religious beliefs. Today, the world is at war because of divergent religious beliefs among ethnic cultures. Don't let your mastermind group go there.

5. *Competence*
Incompetence, gives rise to inferior products and inferior products don't sell, and if you can't sell, your business is doomed. Find your area of competence and operate there, and let your partners also operate in their areas of competence. Confidence comes from competence.

d) *Know who your opponents are*
Your biggest enemies in the game of money are: bad debt and lack of planning. If you spend your income before you plan for it, you are giving room to your enemies. If you borrow money to buy sweets, your enemies will never leave you.
Always learn to protect your assets with insurance policies; you never know what may befall you.
If you can never buy insurance for your asset, your asset is not a smart investment; for instance, can you buy insurance for your pension scheme which can redeem your investment if the currency in which your pension fund exists devalues?
Definitely not, you can never insure your pension fund; therefore it's not a smart investment under conditions which require protection. That's just an example!!

e) Develop an attitude of generosity

Generosity is a money magnet. Give and it shall be given back to you. What is the use of accumulating wealth which you cannot share? Generosity will open up more doors for you.

Are you financially asleep or awake?

Chapter 15

Master your fears and take some risk

Taking the path of least resistance is what makes most rivers crooked

---

*T*here are many kinds of fears: natural fear, the one that prevents you from jumping off a cliff – that's good fear because we still want you around; the fear of God, the one that keeps you from committing sin – that's good fear because we want you to influence generations with your good character.

There is however, one other type of fear that robs many people the experience of a successful and abundant life – the fear of failure; the *"what if it doesn't work"* syndrome *People who always take the easier way out always end up as average and un-inspirational.*

People who create history are those who overcome their fears and take the risks that change their lives completely.

A farmer with seed but keeps saying 'what if it doesn't rain?' may never plant and might therefore never experience the excitement of a harvest.

"What if my investment doesn't yield?" Well, what if it rains, and what if your investment yields your expected results?

Fear is the greatest enemy of your future and is the closest companion of doubt. Fear comes out of doubt, and doubt is a product of ignorance. If fear was given the respect that it demands, the world would never have seen any invention and would never have experienced any revolution.

Some of the greatest inventions of our time are so scary that if the inventors listened to the voice of fear, we would still be living in the Stone Age today.

Imagine what happened when the first aircraft was invented. *"Well, what if it doesn't take off?"* or *"what if it doesn't come down?"* do you expect that these questions were never raised? Someone took the risk of overcoming all these fears; some even died while perfecting the invention and today, you and I can enjoy the benefits for the rest of our lives.

What are your greatest fears? Maybe you are a writer who fears that no one will read your books… maybe you are an artist who fears that your work may never be accepted… maybe you are a musician who fears that your music may never fit into your current society.

Whatever fears you have; remember that no one will ever sing those songs you were meant to sing. No one will ever write those books you were meant to write. No one will ever paint those pictures you were meant to paint – and the greatest tragedy is this: you would have deprived the whole world of experiencing the creative inventions that resided only in you, and all this because of fear.

We live in a world that is interdependent on one another, your gifts and talents were never meant for you, but for the benefit of the human race. However, their manifestation is dependent entirely on you, and you are solely responsible for their development.

Ask yourself these questions:

Was there any need for you to be born?
Did this world really need you?
What would it miss if you hadn't been born?
Ok, now that you have been born, is the world still missing that thing it would have missed if you hadn't been born?
If so, then why are you still here?

Don't allow fear to render you irrelevant to the world in which you live – you were created to rule and not to be ruled.

You were destined for greatness not for littleness.

You were not meant to be insignificant and pass away unnoticed

Your destiny is to leave footprints of where you passed.

One of the greatest ways to overcome fear is to do it afraid – whatever it is you are afraid of, if you make the first step as afraid as you are, you will realize that, that fear will begin to slowly disappear. And the more you do it, the less fear will remain in you, and eventually you will realize that what you were afraid of, didn't even really exist.

Are you financially asleep or awake?

Chapter 16

What is your motivation?

Unmotivated persons can never achieve outstanding results

$\mathscr{D}$onald Trump, one of the most successful real estate businessmen in USA, keeps emphasizing this point:
"To be successful, you must like what you do, even if it's not the most lucrative business you are in, the key is to like what you do."

Lack of motivation in what you do, is the number one reason for failure; it's practically impossible to succeed in business if your business does not inspire and motivate you.

Have you ever wondered why, when a company is advertising for a vacant position, they always say *"we are looking for a self motivated ..."*?
Motivation alone is a great qualification to achieving great results. When management observes that employees are looking de-motivated, they try to implement strategies to motivate their employees again. They introduce things like employee of the month awards; they adjust employees' salaries and so on. The idea is to end up with a motivated work-force that will get the job done.

There is nothing worse than to run a company full of unmotivated employees; the general performance of such a company will go down.
However, motivation must not come from the money you

are getting out of your job or your business, because when you have a down-turn, you will quit. Motivation must spring from within you. You must enjoy doing what you are doing.

I was listening to a local musical radio station; and there was this DJ who was really having a time of his life. The man was enjoying himself and you could tell from the way he was carrying the show. He made a statement during the show and said:

"I never have so much fun doing anything else other than what I am doing right now... and my boss pays me for enjoying myself this much!!"

Clearly, you could tell that this fellow was not in it for the money; he gets the job done because he loves what he does and he's highly motivated about it. It's not about money; it's about you and your destiny.

Unmotivated people are not fun to be around; they are the kind that's always complaining about their job; always looking forward to the knocking off time, and if their boss requests for extra minutes from their time, depression sets in. You don't want to hang around unmotivated people; they have a negative contagious attitude.

If you don't like what you do, quit immediately and find something else that you will like, because if you continue, you will not succeed.

Success without happiness is not true success.
Even happiness itself, is success.

The key word is: find what motivates you and start doing that.

Are you financially asleep or awake?

Chapter 17

A good man leaves an inheritance for his children's children

If your life does not affect anyone, you'll be forgotten before you die

When man was created, he was meant to live forever, never to die, and never to be forgotten. His influence on earth was to last for generations. This was the perfect intention of the creator and it has not changed since.

When man, however, developed bad habits of rebellion against his creator, death was introduced to eliminate the propagation of bad influence on coming generations. This is the whole essence in death – to necessitate a separation between generations and provide a way to allow new life to start again.

If you live a life that has no effect in any way on your first and second generations, you have not lived a worthwhile life.

The idea behind a seed is to keep life in a generation and to take it to the next.

If your life does not affect anyone, you will be forgotten before you die, your remembrance will end at your burial ceremony.

The statements above are very serious statements. Your life was never meant to end at your burial site.

The word 'inherit' means to take after, to genetically copy from, literary to 'clone', to copy your genetic makeup from…

Inheritance has definitely more to do with your genetic makeup and character than the money and property that is passed on to you. In other words, you can leave your houses to your children; you can leave all your money to your grand children and yet not leave yourself into them. Leaving an inheritance to your children goes beyond leaving perishable property to them – it is to leave yourself in them, to never die; so that even after you have gone, you will continue to speak.

You are expected to not only have influence on your generation, but on the second and third generations as well, at the very least. You are to pass on the character of a God fearing man to your next generation; pass on the knowledge of life to them; you are to transfer the *mantle* of excellence to your offspring and allow your good seed to continue.

Well, this sounds like a humongous challenge; a man only has a promise of at least 70 years to live, if he even has enough strength to reach that far – many don't.

How then can you be so good that you can manage to leave an inheritance to your children's children? – And the only credit you get for it is that of a good man.

The biggest obstacle to influencing your first and second generations with your values, character and principles is what I call the *employment syndrome.*

Employment since it started has had many negative effects on a lot of people. To be employed means to be hired and used for a certain task by someone else. There is nothing wrong with being employed; what is wrong is when employment puts a definition of value on your life. In other words, if employment determines your worth and you accept it and live by it, then we have a big problem. This is what causes people to go on strike, demand better pays, hate their jobs and their bosses; primarily because they have unconsciously accepted what value employment has put on them, although deep inside them, they always feel there is something wrong.

Until you begin to personally value yourself, the employment syndrome will define and value you.

If you do not break loose from this definition on your life, you will begin to believe that, that's your true value and you will die within the confines of that definition. When this happens, it is not easy to effectively have influence on your generation and the next generation. The perception of value on your life will determine your capacity to influence generations.

The original reason for employment was and still is: to learn the skills of the trade, to learn to work with people, to learn to work under leadership and to learn to work in a team. The key word is '*learn*'. If you work for any other reason, you may eventually be frustrated. Employment is meant to be a school, a training ground for your future – it's meant to teach you to submit; this is where you pick up principles which will govern you.

The tragedy of employment however, is that for so many, it has become an end instead of a means; it trains you to be perpetually dependent on someone else. When someone else defines your life and you live by that definition, you can only achieve so far – your effect on generations becomes dependent on that definition.

When you realize that the reason you are employed is to learn while you earn, you will direct all your energy to learning ALL that you can so that the definition of value on your life will eventually come only from you.

When you attain this, you can place any value on yourself and people will listen to you. When you fully know who you are and what you can do, you can then share your life confidently with other people – your value will attract people to you – your worth will cause an effect on your generation, your name will become a household name, your history will remain for generations, your life will become a book; and this is how to leave an inheritance to your children's children.

Don't allow your job to define you, give a definition to your job

Are you financially asleep or awake?

Chapter 18

Re-establishing the vision
for your life

It's not over until God says it's over

"*Where there is no vision, the people perish: but he that keepeth the law, happy is he.*" **Pro 29:18**

Other versions say:
"*Where there is no vision, people cast off restraint...*"

*W*ithout a vision of where you want to go and what you want to achieve, your life is lived without rules and without focus. You will accept any offer no matter where it leads you. In other words, nothing restrains you from doing anything.

People who engage in illicit activities do so because they have nothing that restrains them; no vision is so important and passionate enough to them to restrain them from going astray from it. If you are not passionate about something, it's so easy to involve yourself in illegal activities.

A vision in your life will clearly define your goal and will plainly show you what to avoid to get there. Without a vision, nothing is detrimental to your future; because you have no future.

Without a vision, whatever route you take is ok; because there is no definite destiny for you.

Without a vision, there is no success and there is no failure; because you have not defined boundaries.

Without a vision, breathing today is all that matters.

Without a vision, people perish.

If we can find evidence of some breath in you, then your life is not yet over, and you are still needed by this world to contribute the portion of your worth to your generation.

You may have tried many things that didn't succeed and you decided to give up; I would like to give you my final words:

Giving up simply means you are convincing your brain to think that you are a failure.

Giving up means you are accepting defeat as your fate.

Giving up is declaring yourself of no use and of no effect to your society.

A person without a vision, is a person without a road map; it's a person without perception; a person without hope.

What is vision?

It's from the word *vision* where such words like *television* where born. A vision is a picture; a graphical description of your future; it's a painting of how you want to look, who you want to touch, where you want to be, what you want to accomplish... Vision speaks of something in your future.

A vision is a road map to your destiny, and until your last breath, it is vision that's going to lead you to your destiny. Vision gives you a reason to live; and without it, your enthusiasm for life will drain. Vision gives you the power of choice. Only people without vision do anything and everything.

People with vision choose what to do, where to be, who to be with and what time. People with vision are disciplined people.

If your vision is to win a gold medal at the Olympics, you know your diet won't be pop corns, candy and a bowl of ice-cream!! You know what time you need to wake up every morning; you know how long you need to train those muscles…

Vision focuses you in one direction; vision limits your alternatives in life; vision helps you concentrate your efforts.

Have you ever used a convex mirror to focus a ray of light on a spot such as a piece of paper? When the rays of light are totally focused on a spot, that spot begins to gather energy enough to burn the piece of paper or any object on which the rays are focused. This is what vision does. It concentrates your energy to achieving one objective.

What is that one thing for which you'll beg death not to take you until you have achieved it? No matter how many times you have failed, don't rest until you are able to concentrate your rays long enough to burn that piece of paper!!

If you do not have a definite vision that keeps you alive, now is the time to define your vision, make it plain and simple, and *write it down*. Every business is driven by a vision; however, always remember that your life must also be run as a business.

Clearly define your vision; you need to know where you are at, how far to your vision and who you need to associate with to make your vision a reality.

Life unfortunately has millions of choices available for your pick.

Who you are, what you are and where you are, is entirely dependent on the choices you made earlier in life. Without a clear vision, it's a nightmare trying to make the best choice from the options available; if not careful, you may pretty much end up with a frustrated life.

Many people believe in fate, and trust that, if they were meant to be, fate will somehow organizes situations for them to make them become. Logically, this reduces you to a pre-programmed device that goes through some logic until it terminates. Well, you are not a pre-programmed robot that goes through set motions in life.

Most people have misunderstood the message of pre-destination and have gone away thinking their fate has already been decided. The power of choice has been so under-estimated that we often don't give serious attention to the choices we make.

It's not because of fate that you are a drug addict, the first sniff you had, was a decision you made that now defines your life today.

You are going to prison because you decided *to commit a crime; that was never pre-programmed for you by some being sitting somewhere.*

The reason you are with that woman you call your wife or that man you call your husband, is because one day, you decided to get married to that person. That decision was entirely in your hands and nobody else's.
If you ever get divorced, it's not because of fate – you decided once again!!

I do not believe in people who say "*Loose the bird and let it fly, if it was meant to be yours, it will come back to you, if it was never yours, it will never return*"

I believe in knowing what rightfully belongs to you and going for it. I believe in taking control of your life and with the help of God, deciding what to become and where to go tomorrow. People who are lazy wait for things to fall on their laps, and they never do. In other words, you have the power to control your world; Life and death is in your power. With what you choose today, you can forever change your identity.

You are not a failure because you failed one exam in your seventh grade…
You are not a patient because you fail sick last year and spent a week in hospital…
You are not a thief because you stole your friends pencil in class…

You are none of these things because, only with one decision, you can change your IDENTITY.

What are you? Who are you?
You are a voice on which creation is waiting to hear and obey.
You are a king whose word is final.
You are a god who must create your world.

You were born to walk on water just like Jesus. You destiny is to calm the storm and give life to the dead.
You have the power to choose between life and death, between sickness and health, between poverty and wealth, between good and evil.

Choose LIFE.

It's not over until your last breath has left you; not until God says so.

Are you financially asleep or awake?

We want to hear from you. Please share with us on how
this book has blessed you and yours
visit us at http://www.walola.com
or email us on friday@walola.com

Thank you.

About the Author

Friday M. Simfukwe
Business professional, Educator

Friday M. Simfukwe is a business professional whose main thrust and vision is to transform followers into leaders, subjects into masters and mare men into the great people they were really meant to be. A computer systems engineer by design with a bias towards world economics and human development.

He has worked with many young people in universities and colleges teaching them how to discover their purpose and the importance of living a life completely driven by purpose. He's married with four children and currently lives with his family in Lusaka, Zambia.

Chapter 1
Knowledge is more powerful than color

Race and racism in this day and era would be imagined as a non factor; a pillar of an uncivilized culture. However, as remotely ancient as it may sound, our societies are still plagued with these bad eggs and this has a great bearing on the success of an individual. A boy or girl growing up in a racially profiled environment may develop certain undesirable bad instincts and beliefs.

Chapter 2
You can master anything you wish

Whether you realize it or not, your life longs and thrives in success. In any competition, whether you are just playing or it's a matter of life and death, you always want to emerge as the winner. Unfortunately, this does not always happen because you are not yet the master at the game. This chapter gives you a step by step route to mastery which your life so eagerly longs for.

Chapter 3
If you do not sale anything, you'll always be poor

We are all in a buying and selling business if you are not buying, you are selling and if you are not selling, you are buying. To survive in this competitive world, you need to sale. Sale your goods, sale your services, sale your skills Sale!! Sale!! Sale!!

This chapter is about creating value which other people need for you to sale.

Chapter 4
There's only one way to build wealth

This world is full of shoppers and shopaholics; unfortunately, this is not one of the ways to build wealth if it were, 80% of the world would be swimming in wealth (especially women). This chapter focuses on making the reader an investor no matter how little he/she thinks his/her income may be.

Chapter 5
What is the use of being debt free and yet broke

Debt is not always bad but it also is not always good. There's good debt

but there's bad debt. Rich people only go for good debt to make them selves richer; and poor people only go for bad debt which makes them even poorer.

Chapter 6
Repent for the kingdom of heaven has arrived
The word *repent* means change your thinking. Someone once said if you want to change the results you have been getting, you need to change the thoughts you have been thinking. To become successful, you need to adopt the mind-set of a successful man. This chapter focuses on this.

Chapter 7
You were wired for the top
One of the reasons slavery couldn't work and why you hate a boss who's always slumming you down is that your system was engineered to live at the top, to be in control, to rule. In this chapter, we admonish each other on this aspect and together strive to regain our original position the TOP.

Chapter 8
Your future is not in God's hands it's in yours
It's time everyone woke up and realized that tomorrow is in your hands to create. In this chapter we dispel beliefs that no matter what you do or choose as long as God has ordained your future in a certain way, it will come to pass.

Chapter 9
The real purpose of money
It is not up to money to solve problems or answer questions; money does not have power of its own. The ability of money to answer questions and solve problems depends in whose hands it is.

Chapter 10
To do is greater than to have
What you do determines what you have and not the other way round. Knowing about something and doing something about what you know are two different things. Your knowledge is of no effect if it does not influence your actions.

Chapter 11
If you neglect knowledge and despise education, you are abandoning your future
Your future depends on the knowledge and education you acquire today. This chapter deals with issues of effects of ignorance on a people and the

This chapter deals with issues of effects of ignorance on a people and the effects of knowledge contrasted.

Chapter 12
If only I had some capital…
One of the biggest enemies of progress is excuse. "I cannot do this because I do not have that" and the commonest excuse with would-be small business owners is *"I do not have capital"* this chapter deals with this excuse in particular and offers a new approach.

Chapter 13
You should never give your seed
This chapter tries to distinguish the idea of *giving* with the concept of *sowing*. Many times we don't know when to give and when to sow and so when we give, we remain in faith and hope, thinking we sowed. Sowing is equivalent to planting or investing but giving is not.

Chapter 14
Your gift is your wealth
Every person came into this earth packaged to fulfill an assignment. Your gifts and talents are the tools you use to accomplish this assignment. Many people are on wrong assignments and therefore can't excel beyond the average because they are not equipped enough.

Chapter 15
Understanding the value of time
No one will live forever on this earth one day, your end will come; and it is what you'd have done with this all important asset called *time* that will matter after everything. Reorganize before your allocation runs out.

Chapter 16
Know the rules and play the game
Don't be too serious about money; you may die of a heart attack if you are. Take it as a game where you sometimes win and other times you lose. But in every game, it's when you know the rules that you often prevail in the game of money, you need to know the rules to win.

Chapter 17
Master your fears and take some risk
Usually it so happens that the greater the risk, the higher the returns; but a

Man who is always afraid of moving forward always remains at the same point and eventually is wiped out. This chapter challenges the reader to put fear aside and take on the world with confidence.

Chapter 18
What is your motivation?
Achievements are really hard if you are unmotivated and uninterested. Check your motivation thermometer in anything you want to pursue; this alone will provide the propensity to soldier on in times of discouragements and drawbacks.

Chapter 19
A good man leaves an inheritance for his children's children
You were never designed to die that is why you always run away from every appearance of death. But the best way to keep your influence around for generations to come is when you transfer your character into your children's children - into your followers.

Chapter 20
Re-establishing the vision for your life
The world is full of so many alternatives, so many choices; if you are not careful, you can end up sampling around the many alternatives through your entire life. Having a vision for your life eliminates these alternatives and choices it concentrates your life towards achieving your goals. This is what all true masters possess.